9,000 MILES OF FATHERHOOD

Best wishes!

9,000 MILES OF FATHERHOOD

Kirk Millson

PLAIN SIGHT PUBLISHING
An Imprint of Cedar Fort, Inc.
Springville, Utah

ISBN 13: 978-1-4621-1381-1

Published by Plain Sight Publishing, an imprint of Cedar Fort, Inc.,
2373 W. 700 S., Springville, UT 84663
Distributed by Cedar Fort, Inc., www.cedarfort.com

LIBRARY OF CONGRESS CATALOGING-IN-PUBLICATION DATA

Millson, Kirk, 1959- author.
9,000 miles of fatherhood / Kirk Millson.
    pages cm
Summary: Humorous tale of a workaholic and his emotionally estranged 13-year-old son on a four-month road trip to Panama's Darien Gap.
ISBN 978-1-4621-1381-1
1. Fathers and sons. 2. Latin America--Description and travel. I. Title. II. Title: Nine thousand miles of fatherhood.
PS3613.I5914Z46 2014
813'.6--dc23

Cover design by Angela D. Baxter
Cover design © 2014 by Lyle Mortimer
Edited by Daniel Friend and Whitney Lindsley
Typeset by Daniel Friend

Printed in the United States of America

10 9 8 7 6 5 4 3 2 1

Printed on acid-free paper

For Alison

PRAISE FOR 9,000 MILES OF FATHERHOOD

"An insightful page turner . . . a story all dads need to read."

>--Ricky Shetty, DaddyBlogger.com

"Real. Poignant. Captivating. An incredible journey."

>--DadzClub.com

"Millson is comfortable displaying his misjudgments and his parental warts; that is the real charm of this book."

>--Kenny Bodanis, MenGetPregnantToo.com

"Millson's writing flows."

>--Seth Leibowitz, NYC Dads Group

CONTENTS

ONE

There is no road so baleful as the one you are lost on at night in Latin America. The only light is the glow of cigarettes from vacant lots as you roll toward what you are sure is a violent end, and hard-faced men bend low at every stop sign to stare through your windows.

So when a neon hotel sign waves you in from the gloom outside Chihuahua City, you pretend you don't see the yowling hookers working the street in front, even if you *are* traveling with your thirteen-year-old son.

At least that was my story in case this ever got back home. The truth was we'd been blasted by a hundred-degree wind for twelve hours in a car with no AC, and I wouldn't have cared if the harlots were patrolling the rooms. I looked like Charlie Brown's pal Pig-Pen, my tongue was coated with sand, and I might have turned a trick myself for a shower and a cold beer.

I drove through a gate in the security wall and was grateful to see that every room in the long cinder-block building had its own garage. An attendant waved us in, rolled the door down behind us, and opened a peephole, through which I traded two hundred pesos (twenty dollars) for a room key.

The guy rented rooms without ever seeing the patrons, which I thought was odd for the 1.5 seconds I focused on it. Then my mind boomeranged back to the beer sign I had spotted on a little joint up the road. We slipped into the private concrete stairwell that led up to our room, dropped our bags on the first step, and passed through a steel security door into the dim light of the hotel courtyard.

We caught the hookers napping on the way out, but they flew from the shadows like vampires as we returned. The management must have had a rule against the gals roaming the courtyard unescorted, however, because they stopped at the gate and yelled insults as we hurried back to the stairwell entrance.

"Maricón! Maricón!" they shouted, which brought the manager out of his office so fast you might have thought the word meant *fire* instead of *queer*. He yelled something at the women, but he was staring our way as I closed the door behind us.

Our room sat above the garage at the top of a short flight of stairs. The door opened into a hallway, directly across from the bathroom, and the bedroom was a few steps to the left. I set my bag on the floor, grabbed two beers, and went straight for the shower.

"See what's on TV," I called to Peter as I stripped off my sweaty clothes. I turned the tap and drained half of the first can as I waited for the water to warm, and just as I was sliding past the plastic curtain, I froze. Someone was pounding on the door.

I knew from previous travels that unexpected visitors south of the border could really screw up a relaxing evening, and I briefly considered putting my dirty clothes back on. *But there's a locked security door at the bottom of the steps*, I told myself as I wrapped a towel around my waist, stepped from the bathroom, and reached for the doorknob. *It's probably just the maid with some extra pillows.*

The door swung open and the manager barged past. He stopped at the end of the little hallway and studied the bedroom with smug satisfaction. I followed his eyes and muttered a curse as I took my first real look at where I had brought my son for the night. The far wall and ceiling were mirrored and the curtains festooned with silhouettes of naked señoritas. A five-peso condom dispenser was bolted above the nightstand next to the room's only bed, on which Peter reclined in his Scooby-Doo boxers. Beer in hand and jaw on his chest, he was watching two nude dwarves and a Snow White look-alike cavort on a channel that was clearly not Disney.

"You have a boy here," the manager said with an unfriendly smile. "You owe me another two hundred pesos."

We had stumbled into Mexico's version of the No-Tell Motel, typically rented by the hour for a discreet rendezvous between a man and a woman. That I had a boy in the room posed no moral dilemma for the manager; he just figured such twisted behavior ought to cost more.

So much for my promise that this trip would be a positive experience for my son. We had only been out of the country one day and he was already into the beer and porn.

♥ ♥ ♥

To be honest, Peter was not my first concern when I conceived of the trip. To tell the whole ugly truth, I'd have left him home if I could have gotten away with it. But I wasn't exactly thinking straight that day in August 2002 when I decided to drive to the End of the Road.

My side had just lost a two-year court fight for control of the *Salt Lake Tribune*, and the most important allies I had made during a twenty-year career were fired on the spot. I was knocked off the pristine pinnacle of the newspaper business—editorial writer—and tossed back into the refuse-strewn base camp where I had begun my climb—the copy desk. It was the kind of fall that's hard to bounce back from, and I didn't really try. I crawled out of the office and into the nearest bar.

I had a raging hangover the next morning, and after watching blurry want ads pulse across the classified pages for half an hour, I went back downtown for some hair of the dog. I spent the first hour with my head in my hands and my elbows propped on a scratched and water-stained wooden bar, on the same worn vinyl bar stool that I had occupied all too often during my college years.

I glanced at the mirror as I had so often twenty years before, but gone was the fun-loving college kid who was always quick to smile back. The forty-two-year-old version bore a resemblance—curly brown hair tumbling off the sides of a blocky head; the prominent nose, square jaw, and linebacker's shoulders—but there was no smile now and no sparkle in the tired brown eyes. I looked more like the old losers the young guy had tossed out of the place in return for all the beer he could drink.

I drained my glass and tottered out the door, staggering for a moment as the bright desert sunshine struck me blind. I rubbed my eyes until the low brick buildings, wide sidewalks, and even wider asphalt of 200 South materialized amid the glare. I wandered two blocks west and caught the same bus that, until the day before, I had ridden home each day with a briefcase.

When I came through the door, Alison was tossing a salad and frying salmon burgers, looking cute and fit in bright spandex workout clothes still damp from the gym. Tall and gorgeous with long blonde hair, she might have been a leotard model if she hadn't been so top-heavy—in the head, I mean. She was a genetic scientist with a dozen published papers and a chapter in a college textbook. Best of all, she was genuinely nice, and everybody loved her. Alison was a valued employee, a loyal friend, and a wonderful wife, but she did have one blind spot: she never seemed to comprehend how far below her potential she had married.

She leaned in to kiss me as I brushed past, and she didn't say a thing about the stale beer on my breath. She called the kids—Peter and his ten-year-old sister, Hannah—and we gathered at our round kitchen table to eat.

"How was your day?" Alison asked to no one in particular, so no one looked up from the food. "Well, mine was productive," she continued, then launched into a two-minute monologue about some arcane aspect of the latest DNA test she was bringing online. The kids used the time to wolf down their dinners before hopping up with their empty plates as soon as she finished talking.

"Thanks, Mom," Peter said as he raced for the sink. "Yeah, thanks, Mom," Hannah echoed, half a step behind. They could feel the tension in the room, hear it in their mother's voice despite her best efforts to sound chirpy, and they wanted none of it. They disappeared down the stairs.

Alison reached for the salad bowl and shoveled healthy portions onto both our plates.

"How was your day?"

"Fine."

She waited, realized that nothing more was coming, and pressed on.

"My mom says she'll ask her friend to talk to you about an advertising job."

"Mm-hmm," I mumbled as I chewed a piece of burger. I'd sent resumes to every PR firm and ad agency in the city a few years back and couldn't get anyone to return a phone call.

"This time will be different," she continued, reading my mind. "How many resumes do they see from editorial writers?"

Ex-editorial writers, I thought. *Discarded editorial writers.*

"I was also thinking you should apply to law school," she continued, but this time I couldn't bite my tongue.

"A college transcript isn't like a fine wine," I muttered without looking up. "It doesn't get better with age, and my grades would get laughed out of the admissions office."

"Then what are you going to do?" Alison's tone was measured, but in her eyes I saw a flicker of the panic she had been keeping tamped down for the past two days.

I pushed away from the table, leaned over to give her a peck on the cheek, and carried my dishes to the dishwasher.

"I'm going to go to bed."

❦ ❦ ❦

It wasn't that I couldn't bear the thought of not writing opinions. I can't say I had ever truly enjoyed it. Did I think I'd won the lottery when the publisher promoted me after reading a column I'd written on a lark? Sure, who wouldn't? With its daytime hours and weekends off, the job would allow me to see a lot more of my family. I'd get a private office and a hefty raise, and while I would still have deadlines, they'd be nothing compared with those I'd faced while designing and editing the paper's front page. Editorial Writer would have been my dream job if not for those damned editorials.

On my second morning, I took an eye-opening call from a sweet-voiced old lady who wanted to speak with "whoever wrote today's article about the president." Can you imagine my excitement? Here was my first fan, probably calling for an address so she could mail me a box of cookies.

"Why, that was me," I answered, and next to my swollen head the receiver must have looked like Barbie's smartphone. "May I help you?"

"Go to hell!" she snarled.

It turned out that my new job was the literary equivalent of dropping my pants and mooning half the public. As the weeks progressed, the calls were joined by stacks of angry letters, as well as cold shoulders from my former colleagues in the news department. The mayor called to bitch, the attorney general stopped by to moan, and Mitt Romney stormed in with so many lawyers they couldn't fit on one elevator.

I brought a lot of that stress home from the office, which wound up making my kids wish I still worked nights. So all in all, it wasn't a positive move except for one thing: I could hear the pride in Alison's voice when she told people what her husband did for a living.

"Oh, Kirk was just talking about that last week with Milton Friedman," she could say at a party, and the line worked just as well with "the governor," "Senator So and So," or "the ambassador to Fill-in-the-Blank."

Telling people that her husband read page proofs till 1:00 a.m. and bickered over where to put the commas just didn't have the same ring to it.

I had fought this reality with the help of the bottle for two days, but on day three I called the new boss to negotiate my terms of surrender. I would crawl back and become a page-proofer if that's what he wanted, but if I didn't take a few weeks off to get my mind right first, I would surely burn up on reentry—the truth of which the boss seemed well aware.

"Take all the time you need," he said magnanimously, before chuckling and adding, "or at least all the time you can afford."

My hiatus would be unpaid, of course, despite all those years of unused sick leave.

I hung up and walked the half-dozen paces from the kitchen to my daughter's room. Hannah was sitting on her bed next to her 115-pound best friend, an unruly mastiff-mix named Torie.

"Hey, how would you like to go camping for a week in the—"

"No!"

She ignored the wild beats of the dog's tail on her comforter as she calmly closed her book, stood up, and guided me out of the room. The door slammed and the lock clicked.

"Okay, the score is one no and one yes. Peeeter," I called. I walked to the head of the stairs and peered down into the gloom. His bedroom door was open, but the light was off. He was probably out playing someplace with the neighbor kids.

I glanced at the clock—10:30 a.m.—before absently rummaging through the drawer in the kitchen where I kept my stuff. I grabbed my wallet but left the car keys, slipped out the side door, and wandered down the driveway. In truth, I was with Hannah: a week in a leaky tent with a wet dog didn't sound all that appealing. But I had to do something with my time off.

Before I knew it I was at the bus stop and the old No. 52 was rocking into view. I climbed aboard, found a window seat, and watched the trees swish past on our way through Salt Lake's Sugar House neighborhood. A few seats up sat a hobo whom I seemed to see on buses no matter what the time of day. He rode like a master horseman on his favorite steed, his cheek pressed boldly against the window, his skinny frame swaying in graceful harmony with every bump and lean of the vehicle.

I tried it briefly but gave up when the window frame and a pothole conspired to slap a welt on my forehead, but it didn't matter. I wasn't going to spend my hiatus riding buses around town from dawn till dusk. There was, however, something appealing about the mindless travel. What if I just got in the car and started driving and didn't stop until I ran out of road? I sat up straighter and smiled. What if I drove all the way to Panama, to the End of the Road at the edge of the Darién Gap?

My smile broadened, and I had trouble sitting still. I hadn't thought of the Gap in years, which just went to show how deep a rut I had fallen into. I used to be obsessed with that mysterious green void on the map, the only roadless stretch between Tierra del Fuego and the Bering Sea. For me, it recalled the nautical charts of yore where the Atlantic Ocean simply ended next to a well-penned warning to foolish mariners: "Beyond Here Lie Dragons."

I'd first thought of driving there in 1983 when I took my beat-up Dodge Dart deep into Mexico for a two-month adventure with a college buddy. Now I hatched a hasty scheme to go the rest of the way.

My budget would be nine thousand dollars, a sum derived not from a careful assessment of projected expenses but from what I figured I could scrape together on short notice. The trip would last four months because that's how much time there was until Christmas. Whether seventy-five dollars per day was enough for food, lodging, and gas on a nine-thousand-mile road trip was the kind of detail in which I never liked to get bogged down.

In this case, ignorance was bliss. Had I known about the two guys who set a speed record by driving fifteen thousand miles from the tip of Argentina to the top of North America in the late 1980s, I might have concluded that I was woefully underfunded. They spent two years planning and raised three hundred and fifty thousand dollars for their twenty-three-day trip (which included the cost of shipping their truck around the Gap from Colombia to Panama). But I didn't know that, and even if I had, I probably would have chalked up their costs to budget-padding and overthinking. Those guys had filled fat binders with spreadsheets on potential expenses and action plans for every eventuality. My plan was less complex: drift south until I ran out of road, turn around, and drift back north.

I didn't waste a second deciding which vehicle to take. I already owned a 1974 Dart, purchased a few years earlier in a fit of nostalgia for my '83 trip. The car was dependable, roomy, and built like a tank. And as my appalled relatives and friends had pointed out the day I brought it home, it would not draw a second look in the Third World.

I hopped off the bus at the next stop and caught the first one for home. I leaned back against the seat, closed my eyes, and watched myself puffing on a fat Honduran cigar as I bounced down a dirt road toward some trackless Central American beach. I saw myself climb out of the car and slide into a hammock stretched between two graceful palms. I could actually feel the gentle sway thanks to the old bus's well-worn springs, and I might have drifted off to sleep if not for a nagging thought that had been trying to get my attention for several minutes. I had shunted it aside, but it was a persistent cuss, and when it finally penetrated my happy fog, it hit me like a splash of water.

Was it possible that my lovely wife might not share my enthusiasm for this plan? Could it be that she would conclude that a man with no current income should start arranging for one instead of blowing his family's meager savings on a four-month solo vacation? These were sobering questions that were depressingly simple to answer. And even if by some odd coincidence Alison had also lost her mind that morning, our relatives would surely foul things up. They would pound away at her with reason, and that enemy of dreams would crush mine under its boot.

Plan A was dead by the time I stepped off the bus, but my wheels were still turning. If I had any hope of getting out of town, this had to be about more than just me. What the trip really needed was a higher purpose, something like a mind-broadening educational opportunity for a thirteen-year-old boy. I happened to know where I could find one.

Peter was immersed in a handheld video game when I came through the door.

"Hey, buddy," I said, and he jumped. He sat up stiffly and donned a nervous smile.

"Do you want to skip a few months of school and drive to South America?" The question brought the dog galloping down the hall in a tail-wagging, jowl-flapping frenzy.

"Not you," I said as I whacked the animal's solid rump. Peter hadn't budged. In fact, if anything he looked stiffer, and what he saw when he looked at me could not have eased his mind. I had not considered that the boy might not want to go with me, and now that I did I was having trouble holding my face together. My eyes screamed deep concern, but I forced my upper lip to hang in there on its perch above my teeth. Time stopped as we stared without taking a breath. Even the dog was frozen, its jowl curled around a fang in a grimace as macabre as my own.

That my son wasn't jumping at the proposition of spending months in a car with me should not have caught me so off guard. I hadn't been much fun in the years I'd been writing editorials. The nine-to-five shift that had sounded so attractive had morphed into six to five, and I began bringing work—and aggravation—home from the office.

As I huddled over my laptop in the living room each evening, my head was a roiling stew of arguments. Alison, Hannah, and even the dog learned to tiptoe around whenever they saw me muttering at the computer screen, but Peter couldn't do it. He was loud and disruptive—a typical boy—and he caught hell for it. He was barked at so often for interrupting that he stopped trying to talk to me at all, and I was so consumed with work that I didn't notice.

Standing before Peter in the living room that afternoon, I felt my chickens coming home to roost. For a few awful seconds I was certain he was going to blow me off, but then he swallowed hard and whispered, "Okay."

My breath came out in a whoosh. "Great!" I gasped, but at least now my smile was genuine. "That's really great. We're going to have a lot of fun. Why don't you go get packed?"

He tore off with the dog at his heels as I sank onto the couch. That was a close one, and things were going to get tougher when his mother got home. I spent the next half hour fidgeting as I polished my counters to the most obvious objections: Peter will fall further behind in school? Actually, he'll come back far ahead in Spanish and geography. Latin America is dangerous? Not in the cathedrals, museums, and nature preserves that we'll be visiting.

While I paced around the house, Peter was running up and down the staircase. After a few minutes he called me outside to inspect a mound he had created in the driveway. Neatly stacked atop a base of ski boots were a skateboard, five socks (two of which matched), one pair of underwear, and his video game player. His bicycle lay to one side near a Lego model of the Starship Enterprise, atop which perched two dog-eared copies of his favorite periodical: the airline shopping magazine *SkyMall*.

"Uhhhhhhh," I said, but it was all I could manage at the moment. I left him standing uncertainly by his pile and trotted down the driveway to peer up the leafy tunnel of maples that lined our street. The moment of truth was fast approaching, and my mind was racing wildly with a sales pitch that sounded lamer by the second. When I spotted our blue station wagon turning the corner, my mouth went dry, and when Alison stepped out onto the driveway, I lost my nerve. She was so earnest, always so happy to see me. I never could lie to that woman, damn it.

"I took the copy desk job, but I get a leave absence before I have to go back," I began, and as she walked slowly toward the curious mound in our driveway, I added, "That's Peter's idea of packing for a trip."

Her eyebrows arched, and I sighed. "Okay, here's the deal: Central America. Four months in the Dart. It'll take all our savings. I invited Peter because I didn't think you'd let me go alone, but it's probably not a good idea. If he couldn't learn algebra in school, he sure as heck isn't going to learn it by himself in a car."

Alison's gaze moved slowly from Peter's pile to the Dart and back to me. Her face was a strange mix of suppressed emotions that I couldn't decipher, but I didn't like the look of them. I knew my pipe dream was over, and I was starting say that this was the worst idea I'd ever had when she cut me off.

"*I wanna go!*" she wailed.

"You're right, you're ri—Wait. *What?*"

I should have known. If that angel had a vice, it was an itch for adventure only slightly less bedeviling than mine. We had talked for years about moving with the kids to a foreign country to learn a language, but we never could figure out a way to swing it. And we faced the same problem now: if Alison came along, then no one would be home earning money for the mortgage, and the trip would devolve into just another two-week vacation. She knew all that as well as I did.

"I know I can't go," she continued with a sigh. "We can't afford it, and Hannah wouldn't want to miss all that school. And what would we do with the dog? I'm just saying I'm jealous. You guys are going to have a blast."

I couldn't believe my ears. I wrapped her in a bear hug and waltzed her down the driveway. This was really going to happen, provided I got out of town before someone talked some sense into her. She raced off to call her parents, which started the death clock ticking. I figured I had two days.

TWO

Ever wonder where you might pick up a good map of Tegucigalpa on short notice? I hadn't either, and I wound up blowing half a day on that quest before settling on a large-scale atlas of the countries we would transit: Mexico, Guatemala, El Salvador, Honduras, Nicaragua, Costa Rica, and Panama.

I also had to track down Peter's teachers to get his assignments and camp out in the school district office until someone signed off on his long absence. I scoured used bookstores for cheap travel guides, got the car serviced, and sat down with Alison for a few hours to figure out how to juggle the budget after my final paycheck arrived.

That left thirty-seven minutes to pack, and out of fear that we would forget something, we packed everything. We had sleeping bags and pads, a four-man winter tent, water tanks, mosquito nets, three camp chairs, pots and pans, two stoves, and a portable grill. We took backpacks and duffel sacks crammed with every article of clothing we owned, from down parkas to swimsuits. We were ready to bed down anywhere from a glacier to a lowland jungle, and our gear filled the backseat to the headrests.

The Dart was a rolling consignment store, but any concerns I might have had about taking so much visible loot into third-world crime zones were smothered by my fear that I wouldn't get to go at all. I jumped a foot every time the phone rang. My in-laws had been temporarily stunned by the news, as if upon turning a corner they had seen their house on fire, but it wouldn't be long before they hit the alarm.

I waited to tell my mother until the packed car was idling in the driveway.

"Hi, Mom. I'm taking Peter to Central America. We'll be back by Christmas," I rambled as she picked up the phone.

"You're *what?*"

"Gotta go. I'll email you from Mexico."

"*What?! Let me talk to Alis—*"

I hung up and raced outside, where Alison and Hannah were saying good-bye to Peter. I heard the phone ringing as I hugged the gals, so I cut the farewells short and slid behind the wheel. The tailpipe screeched across the asphalt as I backed into the street, and the transmission shuddered before the car lurched ahead.

I kept checking the rearview mirror for the first few minutes, half-expecting to find my in-laws' Subaru on my tail, but when we rolled down the on-ramp onto the interstate I knew we were safe. My mother might yet do something wacky like alert the highway patrol, but it would be a couple of days before she worked herself into that kind of tizzy. By then, we'd be across the Mexican border.

By the time we got up to cruising speed, I was drunk on that wild brand of freedom known only by inmates who have made it over the wall. Do you think I gave a fat rat's ass about my ruined career as I raced through the hot wind like a desert desperado on a stolen horse? Hell no! I was on the lam.

Peter felt it too. Despite the heat, he had migrated away from the open window to the middle of the bench seat, and whenever our eyes met, his giggle pierced the wind's dull roar. We forged a magical, unspoken connection, an understanding as comprehensive as any we had ever shared.

It lasted for an hour, until just north of Nephi I glanced at the gas gauge.

"*Son of a—!*"

I followed that up with a few F-bombs as Peter scooted to the far end of the bench. We had already burned through half a tank, which meant the overloaded car was barely getting twelve miles to the gallon.

There was no talking in that wind, so we didn't even try. Peter spent most of the day curled up on the seat like a sleeping dog, his blond head rising above the window frame only when we rolled to a stop. Then he'd glance at gas pumps before sliding back down to resume his nap unless the station also had a convenience store, which was the only time he became animated. In he'd dash on the pretext of using the bathroom, and a few minutes later I'd go inside to find him mesmerized by a display of truck stop treasures.

After ten long hours, we pulled off the road into the forest near Flagstaff, Arizona. The air was cool on the flanks of the state's highest mountain, Humphreys, which restored just enough energy to set up the tent and slap together some cold-cut sandwiches.

"Hot today," I'd muttered every few minutes. "Freakin' hot."

"Yeah," Peter would agree, then return to his sandwich.

We sat in lawn chairs and stared at the darkening ponderosa pines for the better part of an hour before we had our first conversation. Peter started it.

"Do they have mountain lions in Arizona?" he asked as he squinted at the deepening shadows.

I snorted. "Just hungry ones. Didn't I tell you about Troy getting stalked by that half-starved cougar on the mountain near his house last summer? He and his brother were up all night chucking flaming logs at the thing, and it wouldn't leave. The drought has been tough on the animals in Arizona, but I wouldn't worry about the cats tonight. You're more likely to run into a bear down this low."

Somehow I thought my little tale would be entertaining, but a minute later Peter got up, dragged his sleeping bag out of the tent, and stretched it across the car's bench seat.

"Sheesh. Why are you worried about few man-eaters with me around?" I called, but as he slammed the door, I thought of another amusing statement I had made on another camping trip years before: "I don't have to run faster than a bear," I had declared with a knowing grin. "I just have to run faster than you."

Maybe I wasn't as entertaining as I thought.

♥ ♥ ♥

As we dropped into the Valley of the Sun the next day, the scalding air that poured through our windows made me regret ever mentioning the heat the day before. It was 110 and slightly humid from a recent monsoon rain, and water poured from our bodies as fast as we drank it. As if that weren't enough to put a damper on the day, we were hemorrhaging cash. Gas was up a dime a gallon, and in the heat the Dart burned a quart of oil. Still, I might have held it together had not Peter made an inopportune pronouncement as we rolled past a Tucson mall: "Uh, I might have forgotten to pack some shoes."

"*What?*" I wheeled the car onto the highway shoulder and slammed on the brakes. "Get out!"

There was an ugly second when he must have thought I meant to leave him there, because his blue eyes were wide with alarm. But when I jumped out my side and raced around to the trunk, he was giddy with relief.

"It's okay," he said as I rummaged through the spaces in the mound of gear. "I don't need 'em. I walk pretty good in these flip-flops."

He backed off a couple of steps as I reached for a shoe box crammed up against the fender. A telltale rattle snuffed my hopes that I had found his missing footwear.

"What's this?" I demanded as I shook the box next to my ear. "You remembered your freakin' Legos but forgot your shoes?"

"Maybe we can trade 'em in for sneakers," he rambled nervously. "They might have a store in there where we can trade 'em." He nodded toward the mall.

I half suspected that this was part of some grand plan. The kid was a shopaholic with an encyclopedic knowledge of merchants and merchandise. It was not beyond the realm of possibility that he had researched our route and knew that this mall contained some new store he'd been itching to visit. I was half tempted to drive on and let him shuffle through the next four months in flip-flops, but if he hurt his feet along the way, it would screw up the trip for both of us. I crammed the box back into its spot and slammed the trunk.

"C'mon, let's get this over with," I said.

Peter was a gangly kid, about five foot nine with oversized hands and feet, but he must have felt about three foot nine. As he moved through the mall with elbows pressed defensively to his ribs and his fingers laced in front, he took big, gallomping steps to avoid anyone whose path might come within five feet of his. The giant strides, combined with a pace accelerated by excitement, left his flip-flops dangling precariously from the ends of his size eleven feet, and he had to keep bending down to slide them back on.

He spotted a video game shop and came stumbling back with his flip-flops in one hand.

"I'm going to head up to that shop for a second, okay? You get the shoes."

He took off running, and I was so dismayed by his gall that he was twenty feet away before I found my voice.

"*Hey!*" I bellowed, and all activity in our wing of the mall ceased as suddenly as if I'd hit a switch. Everyone was staring; even a couple of sales girls stuck their heads out of their shops. I smiled weakly at a pair of old ladies whose purses were clutched to their chests as I walked calmly toward my son. I walked calmly, but I wasn't calm, and he wasn't either. He stood with head down and shoulders hunched, like a man bracing for the impact of something falling from the sky.

"Listen, buddy," I whispered, and got him moving with a subtle shove to his back. "I can't get your freakin' shoes unless your freakin' feet are in the freakin' store. Now let's just buy the freakin' things and get back on the freakin' road."

Not that we'd been having fun before, but the ninety-dollar detour was a cloud that we never could shake. We drove the next few hours to Douglas in silence, and the only sound as we ate our dinner of granola bars was the drone of the motel TV.

♥ ♥ ♥

"Get up!" I shook the lump beneath the blanket with my bare right foot. "Up, up, up, up, up, up, up."

Peter's head emerged from his cocoon, his sleepy eyes demanding answers.

"Mexico," I said. I liked the sound so much I said it again and again. Mexico was where this adventure would truly start, where the fun would finally begin.

"Mexico!" I whispered as we drove up to the border.

"Meh-he-co," Peter corrected as we rolled through the gate that separated the towns of Douglas and Agua Prieta.

"You're right, amigo. We're south of the border now, and we have to start speaking their lingo. Meh-he-co, Meh-he-co, Meeeeh-heee-co," I sang to the tune of "Figaro" as we pulled up to the immigration office. "Did I ever tell you how much I love this place?"

Ten minutes later and a hundred bucks poorer, we shuffled out of the building with our papers.

"Freakin' Mexico," I grumbled. "That car permit cost about ten bucks the last time I came here."

Peter made a valiant attempt to revive the festive mood, reprising my "Meh-he-co" song from a few minutes earlier, but I couldn't stop thinking about how many three-dollar hotel rooms and sixty-cent meals a hundred bucks could have bought in 1983. My buddy Troy Gillenwater and I had left the United States with six hundred dollars each and returned two months later with two hundred dollars and a trunk full of souvenirs. If everything in Mexico cost ten times as much this time around, we were in for a short trip.

I drove a few blocks to the town's commercial center, where we bought Cokes in glass bottles and wandered past the shabby storefronts. I had consumed gallons of the stuff on my '83 trip, usually after crawling up to a kiosk half-dead from a long hike back from some wild place, so it held an outlandishly disproportionate spot in my memories. But here on the street of this dingy border town two decades later, it was just a soda I didn't feel like finishing.

"How's your Coke?" I asked Peter, who was wincing from a sizable swig. He gave a quick nod, belched, and took another drink.

I left my half-full bottle on the sidewalk for some lucky street kid and continued walking. Peter was a few steps in front, his head on a swivel as he scanned the store windows on both sides of the street, and he gave such a wide berth to oncoming pedestrians that some stared with disdain. It looked as if this blond gringo couldn't bear to be near a Mexican, but it wasn't that. He was scared of them. Spotting two young men coming our way, he stopped to let me pass, then pulled in so close behind that I could feel his breath on my neck.

When we walked through the door of a general store a few moments later, however, he leapt back into the lead. His apprehension at being surrounded by exotic strangers was forgotten amid the bounty of exotic merchandise. I watched with a mixture of amusement and annoyance as he darted from one display case to another, hefting carved wooden donkeys and caressing porcelain sombreros. What was it about acquiring useless junk that made Peter feel so good?

"What do you think of this?" he asked, holding up a thick leather belt whose beaded message assured the world that the owner was a "Legend of Love." The enormous chrome buckle sported a winking bull with nuts the size of basketballs.

"I think he needs a urologist," I said, squinting at the buckle. Peter's smile started to fade, so I quickly added, "But it's stylish." I reached out and took the belt for a closer examination. "I just think it might be a little too flashy. We don't want to stand out down here, remember? We want to fly under the radar."

Peter stared accusingly at the contents of my shopping cart: two yards of garish red cloth whose frilly fringes were spangled with sparkling doo-dads; half a dozen crucifixes on fake gold chains; a foot-long green-and-red medallion honoring La Virgen de Guadalupe; and a twelve-by-twelve portrait of a weeping Jesus.

"Well, this is different," I said defensively. "What you see here is a camouflage kit. When I put this stuff on the Dart, we'll become invisible."

Peter rolled his eyes and went back to shopping. In the end, he settled on a key ring with the logo of BMW, a car that no one he'd ever met had ever owned and in which until that moment he had never expressed the slightest interest. I couldn't stifle a chuckle when he showed it to me, and his face fell before he shuffled off to wait at the front of the store.

I hung the crucifixes and medallion from the Dart's mirror, pinned the sparkly cloth across the top of the windshield and taped the picture to the back window. Then I stepped away and took a long, admiring look at my work.

"Not bad," I said, and in my mind's eye I saw a different Dart in another dusty border town twenty years before. "We'll fit right in down here."

I noticed Peter staring skeptically at the stream of shiny cars on the road behind us, none of which was sporting so much as a doily on the dash.

"These guys up here try to look like Americans," I explained with more confidence than I felt. "You'll see the real Mexico when we get away from the border."

He looked up and down the street to make sure no one was watching before slipping quickly into his seat.

♥ ♥ ♥

We headed east out of Agua Prieta on a two-lane highway that paralleled the US line, climbing through emerald hills of grass and cacti fat with water from the monsoon rains. We left the Sonoran Desert at the Continental Divide, dropped into the hotter, drier Chihuahuan Desert, and bore southeast to Nuevo Casas Grandes.

"What do you say we get a 'positive experience' out of the way?" I asked as we approached a billboard touting the area's ancient Paquimé Indian ruins.

"Huh?"

"Let's see some old Indian stuff as long as we're here. Your teachers will like that."

But after driving a lot longer than the ten minutes promised by the sign, we found the gates to the archaeological site chained shut.

"My teachers wouldn't like *that*," Peter muttered as I punctuated some observations on Mexican government inefficiency with a few well-placed curses.

"Yeah, well, anyway . . . I still think you should write the report. You could start out by saying 'the Paquimé Indian ruins are shrouded in mystery to this day.'"

I entertained myself with a few more lines from the prospective essay—"The Indians' gatekeepers held random days sacred; I was unable to pick the lock on this mystery"—as I drove back toward the highway, but I must have missed a turn. We wound through ugly hills of sand and brush for what seemed like an hour, taking one wrong turn after another until we hit a dead end.

Our way was blocked by an eight-foot-high earthen berm, above which black pillars of smoke rose from unseen fires. It seemed we had reached the edge of hell, and despite that disturbing revelation, I slipped off my seat belt and opened the door.

"C'mon," I said.

We stepped slowly from the car, climbed cautiously up the slope, and stood in stunned silence before the apocalyptic scene at the top. Dozens of burning pyres rose from a sea of smelly garbage, and a choking blanket of smoke lay thick across the basin. Three silhouettes moved slowly through the fog, stooping now and then to rummage amid the trash. As we moved closer, the trio took shape: a ragged old woman and two filthy little girls, each of whom clutched a soiled bag half-full of the day's "shopping."

Eyes wide with alarm, they watched us approach. Their bags slowly dropped to their sides as their arms went limp with resignation. God only knew who these strangers were, but nothing good could come of their visit. They stood like sheep awaiting slaughter, and one little girl flinched as I reached for my pocket.

"It's okay. Calm down," I said in Spanish. I pulled out a wad of bills and took a half-step toward the woman, but I had a better thought and held it out to Peter. *It will be good for the boy to feel like he's helping these people. It could be one of those life-changing moments when . . .*

Quick as a cobra, he snatched the cash and stuffed it into his pants.

"No, you doofus, it's for them," I whispered. He sheepishly retrieved the bills and offered them to the woman. She slowly raised one bony hand and took the gift, but her eyes lost none of their wariness. What did these hombres intend to buy with the money?

I showed her my palms as we backed away, called out "Good luck" as we topped the berm, and slid back down to the car. Neither of us said a word as we pondered the horror of human beings surviving on the least rancid scraps from a Mexican dump.

We were five miles down the road when I recalled a piece of history that fit so neatly into the day's jigsaw puzzle that it gave me chills. My buddy Troy and his older brother, Gil, had come upon a similar scene in Agua Prieta on Thanksgiving Day 1988. They had responded by founding the Rancho Feliz Charitable Foundation, which has housed, fed, and educated hundreds of Mexican children over the years and today is sending some to college.

To encounter our wretched trash-pickers on a day so dominated by memories of my old pal was a jarring coincidence, and I could see Troy grinning in the passenger seat when I turned to talk about Rancho Feliz. He wore a stupid straw sombrero and let a cigarette dangle unlit from his lips as we raced down the road, laughing as only those without a worry in the world have ever laughed.

But the mists soon cleared, and there sat Peter, staring impassively out his window as I shouted above the wind, and his lack of interest in what I found so compelling drove home a reality I could no longer ignore: I could roll south all year in a Dart tricked out like the one from my fondest memories, but I could never bring back those carefree days. I was an unemployed, middle-aged man in a beater car with a kid I didn't know how to relate to, and the road ahead, so recently shimmering with promise, just seemed long.

THREE

Mornings—before the desert sun turned the Dart into a mobile kiln and when, theoretically at least, we still had a chance to hit our budget—were always the high points of those first days on the road. I rose with some percentage of the exuberance with which I had departed Salt Lake City, enough at least to pretend that we were having fun.

It was a dangerous time because I was prone to decisions I would later regret. Most were small, such as buying breakfast instead of eating our stash of granola bars, but some were more consequential.

"Let's get a monkey," I suggested as we packed up the Dart in Chihuahua City.

"A ma—ma—ma—" Peter's eyes bulged like a strangled toad's.

"Si, señor! We are within spitting distance of one of the greatest open-air markets in the world, and among its many reported marvels is a section featuring exotic beasts. I once read a book that said the Chihuahua City Mercado sells parrots and monkeys, and even baby jaguars."

"Ja—ja—ja—" He sounded like a Swede with Tourette's.

"C'mon," I said and tossed him a granola bar. "Let's get this monkey hunt on the road."

I raised the garage door, slid behind the wheel, and pulled into the gravel lot of the No-Tell Motel. As we passed the office I grinned lasciviously at the day manager, who was craning for a look at the big American pervert he'd heard about from the night guy, and rolled through the gate onto the narrow street.

"Hey, where is downtown?" I shouted in Spanish to a man standing by the road.

"Derecho," he said, turning and pointing the way we were already heading. It was the same thing every Mexican said whenever I asked for directions, and I came to realize that an alternative definition must be "Hell if I know," because more often than not it turned out that they didn't. But this guy did, and before long we hit a big cross street on which several buses were heading in the same direction.

"Must be going downtown," I mumbled as I wheeled in behind the last one.

"It's probably filled with people heading for the market!" Peter chirped. "We'd better get a move on before they snap up all the best monkeys."

I just grunted. Back behind the wheel, I could feel my tank draining fast, especially after I noticed that the Dart's was sitting barely above "E." I scanned the low, gray buildings that stretched into the distance for the flash of green that would herald the distinctive sign of a Pemex gas station, and a shopping spree suddenly didn't seem like such a good idea.

"Say, uh, Peter, how much have we spent so far?" I tried to sound nonchalant, but he could hear the storm brewing. He picked up the notepad on the seat between us, and his lips were moving as he ran his finger down the page.

"Just three hundred and fifty-seven dollars," he said, and as I mentally added the twenty-five dollars we were about to spend on gasoline, I must have winced because Peter started talking fast.

"I think it's closer to three hundred and fifty-six. I wrote down a pack of gum I bought with my own money." He snatched a pencil off the dash and erased the offending figure from the page.

I forced a sickly smile but didn't say anything. As much as I wanted to share his excitement over removing thirty-five cents from the balance sheet, I knew we were in trouble. We were blowing through 120 dollars a day, a rate that would have me back on the night shift before Halloween.

Minutes later as I watched the pesos fly past on the digital gas pump, I was struck by a nasty realization. In the United States, gas was a dollar sixty a gallon; here it was six pesos per liter, or about two thirty-five a gallon. So that 120-dollars-a-day figure was going to grow.

"How many miles to the gallon did we get yesterday?" I asked.

"About fifteen," Peter replied immediately. With nothing on TV this morning but randy dwarves, he'd had nothing better to do than work it out.

"We've come about 1,200 miles, which leaves roughly 7,800 to go," I began, and Peter got his pen and pad ready. "What's our total gas bill if we average two thirty-five a gallon?"

With a monkey hanging in the balance, he began scribbling furiously.

I handed the attendant four hundred-peso bills, and he returned a few coins. I eased onto the road and cringed as the tailpipe shrieked across the lip of the gas station lot. It sounded like a banshee screaming "Iiiiiiiiidiot!"—reminding me again of all the junk we were hauling.

Traffic got heavy as we approached downtown. The road widened into a four-lane boulevard with a raised concrete divider on which adults and children dressed for work and school waited for a break in the stream of cars. Both curbs were also lined with people, and they all leaned forward like sprinters at the starting line.

It was a nerve-racking drive, and it took every bit of concentration I could muster to ignore the many feints of the impatient pedestrians. The only way to survive this game of chicken was not to blink.

"Twelve thousand two hundred and twenty dollars," Peter announced, and I blinked. Choked, actually. As my foot slipped off the gas, the mob sensed weakness and leapt off the curb en masse. I had to stomp the brakes to avoid a massacre, which was beyond the comprehension of the guy behind me. He plowed into our back end a full second after I screeched to a stop.

All I saw in the rearview mirror was the crumpled top of a blue hood protruding from a cloud of steam. I froze, wondering whether the driver of such a devastated vehicle was dead or just horribly maimed. But when he hopped out shaking his fist I considered that question adequately answered. I laid on the horn and floored it, subjecting the pedestrians to an agility test that I'm happy to report they all passed with flying colors.

Peter watched the receding bedlam through the back window, and when he swung around, his expression was a mixture of scorn and fear. Half said, "This hypocrite has told me to respect the law my whole life, and now he's fleeing the scene of an accident." The other half said, "Dad's lost his mind."

I took a sliding right turn onto the first cross street, hung a quick left, and raced into a leafy residential area. After a few more turns, I squealed to a stop next to a curb and jumped out.

I was almost afraid to look at the car's rear end as we fled up the sidewalk, but I couldn't resist. The sight stopped me in my tracks. Not only was there not a dent on the mighty Dart, there wasn't a scratch. The guy must have made a direct hit on the bumper, which was a veritable battering ram of solid American steel.

"What a car!" I crowed to Peter, but he was still watching me through narrowed lids. I pointed at the bumper. "Look, no marks. The cops won't have any idea we were in that crash. There's nothing really to draw attention to . . ."

Peter turned around and stared up the street.

"Aw, to hell with it. Let's go." I passed him and led the way at a good clip up the sidewalk. I wasn't sure where we were or where we were heading, but I figured it was best to stay off the street for a while. The car might not be damaged, but those garish decorations would stick in the mind of anyone who had seen us. It seemed that Mexicans had outgrown the fad in the past twenty years, and their cars were nicer too. The owners of the shiny BMWs and Jettas that had passed us on the drive from the border had looked down their noses at our beater car with its odd ornamentation. Instead of blending in, we stuck out like los Beverly Hillbillies.

"Twelve hundred and twenty-two, I'll bet," I said as we turned a corner onto another residential street.

"Huh?"

"One thousand, two hundred, twenty-two dollars—not $12,220. I think you missed a decimal."

"Huh?"

"The gas bill."

"Oh. Yeah."

We walked the next few blocks in silence until we chanced upon a cathedral with a park-like courtyard. We found an empty bench and took a seat. Peter seemed stunned.

"The police down here aren't like at home," I said quietly, and he just stared at his knees. "I had to run. If I had waited back there, they'd have blamed the wreck on me."

Silence.

"I would have had to pay a huge bribe."

"And we can't afford that," he replied after a few seconds.

"Yes! Exactly!" I was relieved he had finally understood the dilemma, but I still felt guilty. The last three days were by far the most time I had spent with Peter in years, and the highlights were a hooker hotel and a hit-and-run. I picked at the cuticle on my thumb for a few minutes as I searched for something to say, but I couldn't think of anything. Finally I just stood up.

"C'mon, let's get out of here."

I reached the sidewalk first, intent on retracing our steps to the car, but I hesitated. A well-dressed older woman was ambling our way, and I motioned for Peter to hold still.

"Señora," I began. "Please . . ." I wracked my brain for the correct combination of Spanish words while she stared uncertainly. "Where is the big market?"

"Derecho," she said, half turning and pointing back the way she had come.

"I knew it," I muttered and was about to turn around when my brain jam suddenly broke loose. "Monos!" I cried, and I was so amazed that I had pulled the word for *monkey* out of my sombrero that I didn't immediately follow up with something that might give it some rational context. I smiled stupidly. The woman's face began to crinkle, so I stumbled on. "Where can I buy monkeys?"

The woman flinched and took a quick step sideways, looked me up and down with troubled eyes, and hurried across the street.

"I think that book might have been wrong about the monkeys," I said as we watched her trot up the far sidewalk. Or maybe it was just out of date. When I thought about it, the thing had smelled pretty musty when I had pulled it from the University of Utah library shelf twenty years earlier.

Peter just grunted. Whether Chihuahuan monkeys existed or not, he'd already figured out he wasn't getting one. He fell in behind me and trudged silently back to the car.

❦ ❦ ❦

We drove south for hours through hot fields of wheat and cotton, chilis and alfalfa. We passed through Delicias and saw a colossal clock tower that would have been a better fit in Switzerland. We stopped for a plate of beans and tortillas in Santa Rosalía de Camargo near its iconic whitewashed mission and blew through affluent Ciudad Jimenez with its flashy modern architecture and boulevards lined with stately trees. All the while I thought about the quiet kid in the passenger seat.

Peter hadn't always been so withdrawn. He used to chatter non-stop on our many camping trips, which started when I stuffed the little two-year-old into the top of my backpack and hiked into Utah's canyon country. He was also fearless then, nothing like the timid oddball who ducked behind me at the sight of Mexican strangers. He led us up an icy sandstone butte one night in mid-December in cold so biting we had to rotate like pigs on spits in front of a fire. On another trip, we ran out of water and survived for two days on the skiffs of snow we scraped from the shade of junipers. Peter thought it was a blast. Of course, we hadn't been camping in years. And come to think of it, we hadn't really had what could be described as a conversation in . . . sheesh, I couldn't remember.

"Well, no time like the present," I muttered.

"What?" Peter yelled above the wind.

"One second." I wasn't ready because I hadn't thought about how to start. I searched the car for inspiration before settling on the one thing that no thirteen-year-old boy in his right mind would ever feel like talking about: a worn paperback version of *Jonathan Livingston Seagull* that his English teacher had sent along. I got what I had coming.

"How's the book?" I yelled.

"Good."

"What's it about?"

"A bird."

"A seagull, right?"

"Yeah."

"What's he do?"

"He flies."

"Sounds fascinating."

A restaurant mercifully appeared on the roadside, and I wheeled into the sandy parking lot.

♥ ♥ ♥

I invented jobs to get Peter talking, if only in one- or two-word bursts. Most of the tasks were busywork, such as converting the kilometers on highway signs into miles or assembling the correct change for tolls. And since the jobs were dull and mostly unimportant, we both soon lost interest. When we crossed into the relatively backward state of Durango, however, Peter accepted a position worthy of his attention: *tope* spotter. Topes (toh-pays) were concrete speed bumps so tall and steep that our muffler dragged no matter how slowly I crept over them.

I hit the first one at twenty miles per hour after missing the warning sign, bouncing Peter out of his third nap of the morning and dumping him onto the floor. His head and shoulders rested on the torn green carpet, and his chin was mashed into his chest. His feet waved like drunken giraffes around the headrest, and his eyes burned with indignation. It was a funny sight, and I started to chuckle. But then he grumbled, "You drive like Unk," and I went stiff.

"Unk" was my father, an aging man of inexhaustible vanity who had tried to persuade his grandchildren to call him "uncle" so as not to betray his true age to the women of the world. When it morphed into "Unk," which sounded like the kind of oafish ghoul who would steal body parts for Dr. Frankenstein, he tried to walk it back. But it was too late.

Though Unk was hardworking and honest, his good traits were lost in a billow of road dust for anyone who had ever had the misfortune of sharing his car. Embittered by years of stomach-churning travel with the man, I believed no greater menace had ever slid behind the wheel.

It was the perfect insult conjured with impressive alacrity, and my gut reaction was to return fire. I glanced repeatedly between Peter and the road as I worked on an appropriate comeback, something involving booster seats and bike helmets and special classes for kids too dim to use their seat belt. But I could see him bracing for it, so I held back. Unless I wanted the past three awkward days to run on a loop for the next few months, I probably needed to lay off the sarcasm.

"Naw, Unk would have hit that thing at eighty-five," I said with a forced smile. "If he were driving, you'd be right side up because the car would be upside down. Now c'mon, get up and help me keep an eye out for these freakin' speed bumps."

I offered my hand, and he pulled himself back onto the seat, and for the rest of the trip he didn't miss a tope—which is saying something. Even the sleepiest little towns had at least two, one at either end, and some of the more industrious had a dozen or more at which peddlers would wait with their goods.

"Toh-pay!" Peter would yell, and a moment later a crowd would descend on the car with water or candy or random items like tin colanders and bags of pink plastic curlers. The people would laugh as our tailpipe shrieked across the speed bump, and a few seconds later Peter would call out, "Toh-pay," and the scene would be repeated with a different group.

It was tedious going, and a two-mile town could put a real dent in the travel schedule. Unfortunately, the farther south we drove, the more we encountered. One state had built all of its tollbooths for its planned north–south highway but only a few miles of new road. A half mile after each booth, the four-lane turnpike would end at a barricade, and traffic would be shunted onto a narrow strip of weed-lined asphalt. Shortly before the next booth, traffic would be funneled back onto whatever little stretch of four-lane the state had completed.

That was maddening enough, but small towns sometimes put up barricades on perfectly fine stretches of highway to force traffic to detour through their business districts. Late in the day, we flew around a blind curve that abruptly ended at a line of oil drums on which someone had attached a board with a hand-drawn arrow. There was no time to stop, so I wrenched the wheel left and skidded onto a narrow strip of asphalt that immediately curved back to the right.

"Toh-paaaaaaay!" Peter screamed as the car went airborne. We hit the ground at a slant in a cloud of burning rubber and slid to a halt against another bump fifty feet farther on. I was staring straight ahead with my white knuckles locked on the steering wheel when I caught movement out of the corner of my eye.

"Do you want to buy a tamale?" asked a woman so short her head barely cleared the bottom of the window frame. Her nervous eyes never left the road behind us. "Or a comb, maybe?"

But before I could answer, her eyes bugged out, and she scampered back to the sidewalk. I heard the desperate squeal of skidding tires on the curve behind us, and I goosed the Dart into a bucking, clanking transit of the tope without a glance at my rearview mirror. When I finally dared to look, as we rolled slowly away from that little den of ruthless capitalism, the tamale woman was ambling up to another dazed customer.

Peter's trembling hands were clutching the vinyl dash and he was breathing hard.

"Is *that* how Unk drives?"

I tried to smile, but I couldn't quite manage it. "Only when he has some time to kill," I said. "He's worse when he's in a hurry."

FOUR

Our fourth day on the road was so blistering I figured it must be payback for all my griping about the first three. Someone in hell was turning up the thermostat every time I complained, so I zipped my cracked lip. By noon my tongue was too cooked to form words anyway.

We hit Torreón at dusk, so hot and dusty and tired that I pulled into the first motel I saw. Large swaths of yellow plaster had crumbled away from the cinder block edifice, giving it the look of a place that had just come through the blitzkrieg. Our room's only window had a torn screen, through which noise and exhaust from the nearby boulevard wafted in on a sweltering breeze. There was one small bed with a sheet so suspiciously mottled that we covered it with beach towels before daring to climb on. A headless pipe in the moldy shower produced no water, and a vile hole in the concrete floor passed for a toilet.

The wretched place was beyond the dubious redemption offered by a series of unlikely amenities—mirrored ceiling, condom dispenser, a black-and-white TV whose sole channel served up soundless porn—which marked it as a low-budget knock-off of a No-Tell Motel.

Peter made a beeline for the bathroom, which was missing its door. When he returned I was perched on the edge of a chair, peering past the curtain at the dimly lit parking lot. I was intent on spotting the world's ugliest hooker, so it didn't immediately register that Peter had crawled onto the bed and plumped a pillow against the wall. When I did glance over, his eyes dropped quickly to his lap. The faintest hint of a smirk crossed his lips, which would have raised my suspicions had I not been so preoccupied.

I had read stories on the AP foreign wire about a giant lead smelter that continually coated Torreón in toxic dust, and I was expecting to see a woman of obvious brain impairment, if not a cyclops, lurch out of a car and into one of the rooms. But I had to abandon my quest when another toxic cloud wafted out of the bathroom.

"Good sweet mother of . . ." I stumbled to the door ". . . Sainted Baby Buddha . . ." and staggered into the parking lot, where fumes from the adjacent roadway suddenly smelled like rose perfume.

I breathed in deeply and rubbed my watery eyes for a moment before a din cut through the fog. It was a vaguely familiar sound, one I used to know well but hadn't heard in years. Peter had dissolved in belly laughs, the kind that leave you breathless and clutching an abdomen so sore you feel like you've been punched.

He was legless for ten minutes after the air cleared and I ventured back inside. For the rest of the night, whenever our eyes met he would double over in a fit of giggles.

It was really the first fun he'd had on the trip, and it seemed that we had finally stumbled across something on which to build. A foundation of feces might sound wobbly, but it would have to do.

Peter recognized the opportunity. When he stopped laughing, he ran out to the car and returned with his notebook. He tallied up the day's expenses while I braced myself for the damage, and when he called "two hundred dollars," my eyes bugged out so far he started giggling again.

"Just kidding," he said quickly. "It was really only 125 dollars. I figured you'd feel better if you thought it was more and then heard less."

That's a dangerous game, kid, I thought as I massaged my eyelids. It felt like I had pulled something deep in my skull. As the shock wore off, however, I realized he was right. I did feel better, though the fact that we were still fifty dollars over our daily budget had me plenty worried.

"We can't spend four months on the road," I began. "We'll never make it. We need to stay in one place for a while until we can stop the bleeding."

I retrieved the guidebook from the car, and we spent the next hour figuring out where to go. The first half was a waste because, absent any parameters, Peter went straight for the sections with the five-star beach hotels and expensive scuba packages. When I suggested some limits—ten-dollar hotel rooms, three-dollar dinners—our choices narrowed fast. We discussed the merits of Nicaragua, Honduras, and Guatemala, which I was leaning toward until Peter surprised me with an inspired choice.

"What about this place?" he said, pointing to a section on Oaxaca, Mexico.

Pronounced "Wa-ha-ka," it was the capital of a poor southern state of the same name. Founded in the 1500s, it was built around a charming colonial center, though the main attraction for Peter was a three-line blurb about a restaurant that served octopus soup. I liked the cheap prices at the town's many language schools, which would give us something productive to do while we spent a few weeks getting back on budget.

It was nice to have made such an important decision together and nicer still to have talked for so long. Unfortunately, that night in the foul hotel was the emotional apex of our first week in Mexico. By late morning the next day, our foundation was back in the toilet.

At lunch in Zacatecas, Peter suddenly stood up, smacked his sides, and screamed. I thought he'd swallowed a bad frijole, but the trouble lay on the outside of his bony frame. He realized he had left his money belt with all his savings—105 dollars—on the sink in the hotel bathroom, and the realization that there would be no shopping for useless junk in exotic markets was a devastating blow.

Of course he wanted to turn around and drive four hours back to the hotel, but I figured that if the manager was honest, we could handle the recovery by phone from Oaxaca. If the manager wasn't honest, then going back would be a waste of time, gas, and highway tolls.

The discovery put a damper on the day that we could never shake. My best attempt came late that afternoon, and it was a disaster. Just north of Mexico City, I gave Peter another job, navigator, whose sole responsibility was to find us a way around that traffic-choked metropolis.

"We can go east toward Puebla or west to Toluca," I said as he unfolded the map. "I don't care which. Just tell me which exit to take."

I gave him the map without considering whether he had ever read one, which it turned out he hadn't. An hour later I fired him as we were swept into the heart of the world's biggest cesspool in the middle of a six-lane river of cars.

It was my fault and I knew it, but that didn't stop me from cussing like a character from *Deadwood*. That made Peter feel worse, which soured my mood even more as we crept along in an epic traffic jam. We had arrived at rush hour, though I'm not sure there is ever a good time to drive into a city of twenty-one million people. We played stop-and-go for two hours on a perimeter highway until I made the mistake of getting off to check the map myself. Within a minute, flashing blue lights filled my rearview mirror.

The cops were driving a tow truck, and one guy hopped out while the other parked their rig out of sight around a corner. When the driver joined his partner, I stepped out into a drizzling rain. I noticed that they had taken off their badges and name tags, but the black grips of their pistols still jutted conspicuously from holsters on their hips.

My Spanish at the time was passable, but it still took me a while to understand my "crime."

"You have a green car," said the first cop.

"Uhhhhhhh . . . well . . . hmmm." What else could I say?

The second cop led me over to the front of the car, where he squatted and pointed to a number 6 on my license plate. "This is bad," he said, and though I was aching to tell him that a 6 is only bad when it comes in threes, I bit my tongue. I watched silently as the cops conferred, certain that I would be rewarded at any moment with a clarification.

And sure enough, when the first cop looked up I saw a flash of reason in his eyes. I awaited his words like a scribe at the knee of Socrates.

"The car is green and the license plate has a 6," he explained, and I muttered a few of my own observations which, though in English, carried a tone the men couldn't miss. The first cop backed off with a frown to brainstorm again with his partner.

"What's going on, Dad?"

Peter's head was sticking out of the window. I walked over and leaned on the sill.

"This is why I drove away after the wreck in Chihuahua City instead of waiting for the cops," I explained. "I'm about to get a fine."

"But we didn't do anything!" he howled.

The cops stopped talking.

"Just roll up the window and stay quiet," I said. "I'll take care of this."

I walked back and resumed negotiations, and after another few frustrating minutes I understood. As an anti-pollution measure, Mexico City issues license plates with numbers that indicate which days vehicles of certain colors must stay off the roads. That Utah plates weren't designed for the system and thus conceivably could be in violation 24/7 was no excuse. I was driving a green car with a 6—and on a Thursday, no less!—which made me a desperate criminal.

I should have saved time and just paid the bribe, but I was tired and angry. We had eaten nothing but beans and tortillas the past two days, and I hated to pass the savings along to these miscreants. So I argued. I played dumb by speaking English spiced with Russian cusswords for five straight minutes. As a last resort, I tried bluffing them with my newspaper ID, explaining solemnly that I was writing a story that would be seen by a million people in Mexico and the United States. I might even send a copy to their president, Vicente Fox.

"And how do you spell your names?" I asked, though I didn't have anything to write with.

The second cop gave the ID a disdainful glance before handing it back without a word.

"The fine is one thousand dollars," said the first one, a cocky little chain-smoking rooster whose "You're screwed" smirk made me want to wring his neck. "If you don't pay, we will have to take your car."

"Take it," I said, and I was half serious. I was so sick of the money-sucking heap at that moment that I was ready to walk away. But I didn't want those crooks to have it, so I added a caveat: "But first I want to talk to your boss."

The cops chattered back and forth for a few minutes before the bigger one walked off to stand under an awning out of the rain. The little one took another run at it.

"You don't want us to take your car," he said, to which I replied, "I want to go to the station and talk with someone who speaks English."

"You can't do that," the little cop snarled, and his buddy shouted something I didn't catch. Things were coming to a boil, and then a flash to my left blew the top right off the kettle. Peter had snapped a photo of a shakedown by two cops who had gone to the trouble to take off their IDs and hide their vehicle—and I had just told them I was a reporter.

The little cop's head snapped toward the car, and as his "You're screwed" smirk morphed into an "I'm screwed" look of panic, he dropped his cigarette and slid his hand onto the butt of his pistol. I followed his eyes and saw Peter's triumphant grin change to a grimace of fear in one beat of my heart. The other cop screamed, "Get out of the car!" as he sprinted toward Peter's door, and my own fear put wings on my feet. I covered the three yards to the door well ahead of the sprinter and before the little cop had finished his second step.

My adrenaline was raging, which made it easy to pull off an acting job that saved my camera, though at the time I believed much more was at stake. I had read wire stories about Mexico City cops murdering people to cover up robberies. If these guys took all our money, hooked up our car, and drove to the dump to burn us with the evidence, who would ever be the wiser?

So I ripped open Peter's door and yanked him out. The big cop grabbed my arm, but I shook him off, seized the lip of the car's roof, and fired a blast of 120-decibel gibberish over the top of Peter's head. I snatched the camera from his hand, shook it theatrically in his face, and pitched it violently into the back. Finally, I pushed Peter into his seat, tapped down the lock, and slammed the door.

The second cop began pulling on the handle of the locked back door, but I dismissively waved one hand as I dug the other into my pocket.

"Don't worry," I gasped. I was breathing as if I had just sprinted four hundred yards. "The camera . . . is broken." I coughed. "It is just a game for the boy."

I held out 550 crumpled pesos. "Take it. It's all I have."

The naked avarice with which the little one snatched the money told me I had grossly overpaid. The cops trotted back to their truck without another word and I swayed on jelly knees for a few seconds before I could walk to my door.

Now that Peter was safe, I really felt like murdering him, though I didn't say a word as I slid onto my seat. My stomach was churning, and I was sure I was going to be sick. I rested my head on the steering wheel until the nausea passed.

"Did you see how mad those guys got?" Peter asked, and he giggled nervously.

I rolled my forehead until my cheek lay atop the far left curve of the wheel and stared until he turned away.

It had stopped drizzling, and the traffic had lightened a little. I pulled away from the curb and drove back toward the freeway, but we hadn't gone two blocks before the blue flashing lights of another cop car filled my rearview.

"You have got to be freakin' kidding me," I moaned as I pulled over to the curb. I hopped out but abruptly leaned back inside.

"Touch that camera and I'll shoot you myself."

This cop was a big guy with a friendly smile. He asked all about the Dart, checked out the engine, commiserated with me about the high price of gasoline, happily pocketed a twenty-dollar bribe and drove away yelling, "Good luck, friend!"

We had just blown through a day's budget in five minutes and I was in a full panic. What if this went on all night? There had to be a hundred thousand cops in this megalopolis. How many would rob us in the hours it took to find our way out of town? And what if the first cops were on the radio now directing their buddies to the rolling American cash machine? We had to get moving, but we also had to hide.

I took the first side street, and we wound our way through ever-dingier barrios. It seemed prudent to go to where the poor people lived because a crooked cop wouldn't waste his time "patrolling" where there was no money to steal. We climbed narrow dirt streets past plywood shacks with roofs of corrugated metal, and the eyes of the scroungy inhabitants flashed like a cat's at the sight of a mouse. But they didn't worry me half as much as Mexico City's finest.

Peter laid the map upside down across his lap and began calling out instructions with irritating frequency. He was desperate to make amends, and I appreciated the sentiment, so for a while I ignored him. But when he yelled "Turn left" at the mouth of one too many cul-de-sacs, I snatched the map from his lap and tossed it into the back.

We crested a mountain not long after passing the final shanties and zigzagged down the back side into the night. Peter sat stiffly in the car for the final exhausting hours of the drive, staring forlornly at nothing in the soft green glow of the dashboard lights, and I knew he was wishing he were home. The trip had turned out to be a stressful grind for both of us, and after nearly a week together, our relationship was as tense as ever.

FIVE

Our mastiff mix, Torie, had six brain cells, five of which were usually engaged in fervent prayers for food. When she wanted to go outside, however, she could concentrate the meager collection into a single beam that would issue from her brown eyes to poke some primitive receptor in my brain with tenacious repetition. Even dead asleep, I was helpless to impede the intrusion. I would awaken to find her staring like Uri Geller trying to bend a spoon.

I felt the beam the morning after our Mexico City debacle, and as consciousness took hold, I realized I was back in Salt Lake City. The how of it was unclear. All I knew was that my first sight when I opened my eyes would be the big mutt's black nose just inches from my own. Some people might have found comfort in the knowledge that they were in their own home instead of an STD incubator off some noisy Mexican highway, but not me. The past few days had been mostly miserable, but I wouldn't have traded them for a single night in the old newsroom. As I lay there thinking about my next twenty years in the ink mines, the cold hand of dejection reached up from my gut and squeezed my eyelids tighter.

I wanted to sleep for a couple of days, but concerned that Torie's overburdened brain would ignite and leave her dumber than she already was, I forced my eyes to open. There lay Peter, head on his pillow, staring just like the dog. His eyes narrowed with unease before he flashed a quick smile of relief, a perfect reflection of my own emotional whiplash.

My trip wasn't over! And from the looks of the boy, he wasn't ready to go home either. He didn't seem to be harboring any grudges about the past few days. In fact, he was in as good a mood as I had seen all week.

"Good morning!" he chirped.

"Mornin'."

He sat up, and I noted that he was already dressed. For the past few mornings I'd had to shake him awake, and he had shuffled half-conscious from hotel room to car. But today he was waiting for me. Something was up.

"What time do you think people get to work around here?" he asked, trying to sound nonchalant.

"Huh? I dunno, probably nine," I answered, thoroughly perplexed. He frowned, which left me further flummoxed. "What's wrong? Who cares? What time is it anyway?"

"Eight. Well, almost."

I checked my watch. "Almost 7:25," I muttered, and I was about to ask what the big freakin' rush was all about when it hit me. The money belt! We had talked about getting the Oaxaca tourist office to call the hotel in Torreón. I had forgotten all about it because I knew it was hopeless, but Peter probably hadn't thought about much else in the past two days.

"Well, it's pretty early. How about we catch a bus downtown for some breakfast first? I know they don't serve any here."

"Here" was our hotel on the outskirts of Oaxaca. It was a charming place featuring manicured grounds and pleasant whitewashed buildings with faux-green shutters. The curtains were plain white linen, the walls a cheery yellow, and every window had a bright red flower box trailing lavender verbena. Except for the cable porn and hookers ducking in and out of the rooms, the place was downright wholesome.

It was the Hilton of No-Tell Motels, but at twenty dollars a day, the place didn't fit our long-term budget. After we stopped by the tourist office, our next quest would be finding a cheaper place to live.

The bus downtown dropped us across from the Zocalo, a pretty park that serves as the geographical and spiritual heart of the city. Flanked by regal remnants of the Spanish colonial era and dotted with welcoming benches beneath giant shade trees, the Zocalo was an enchanting change from the ugly, hectic Mexico with which we had become so intimately acquainted.

It felt so good to be off the road! I had no place to be and nothing to do, and I bobbed atop that intoxicating wave that breaks on the first day of a long-awaited vacation. For a second I even considered having a celebratory margarita just to keep the buzz going, but as I looked around for a cantina, I spotted a familiar blond head and thought, *Oh yeah*.

We got an outdoor table at a café near the towering cathedral and cleaned our plates of rice and eggs in awkward silence. Fortunately, there was enough going on that we could pretend to be distracted by watching the people. A group of men in dress pants and polo shirts stood nearby, arguing around a bench with a shoe shiner sporting the jersey of the Cruz Azul soccer club. With all the arm-waving and shouting, I was expecting a good brawl, but the group suddenly exploded in back-slapping laughter. Young lovers strolled hand in hand near the gazebo, and a clutch of pretty girls in Catholic school uniforms swayed around a long-haired young man strumming a guitar for pocket change.

We also spotted a collection of the most wretched beggars this side of Calcutta, including an old blind woman with no arms or legs. Presumably, whoever had set her out there in the morning would collect her later in the day, but in the meantime she had to sit like Buddha, helpless to stop the maddening parade of flies running across her face. How could she just sit there and take it? How could she not roll on the ground and fill the park with shrieks of impotent rage?

We paid our bill and hustled over with the change. If nothing else, business was good for the unfortunate woman. People shuffled forward in a line like supplicants to drop a few pesos in her can, and almost everyone kept their eyes averted while they did it. One young tourist, however, made the mistake of staring full upon the woman as he leaned in with his coins, and it stopped him dead. The sight of all those hairy blue abdomens speckling that pathetic brown face was dangerously mesmerizing, and it was a good three seconds before he moved again. When he did, it was with the deliberate languor of a coiling snake, and you could almost hear him think: "Just one more step, slow and easy, and I can smack that big one right off her forehead."

A nervous cough broke the fellow's trance. As he cocked his head and saw the concerned stares of a half-dozen people, it must have occurred to him that his humanitarian gesture had an excellent chance of being misinterpreted. He backed away as coolly as one can when caught in the act of attacking a crippled blind grandmother and scuttled off to the other side of the park.

We weren't far behind. Peter had a nose for souvenirs, and he had sniffed them out by watching which direction the shoppers came from. A lot of the stuff on the blankets lining the park's main sidewalk was Chinese junk right off the boat—cheap jewelry, pocket knives, plastic lighters—but there were also colorful wooden animals, pottery, and other crafts for which Oaxaca was known. I took a seat on a nearby bench to watch the show, which had all the elements of a classic: loads of exotic merchandise, a young shopaholic and—for added drama—not a peso in his pockets.

The extravagant grins on the garishly painted carvings were no match for Peter's as he tested the weight of one after another. It wasn't long before he had narrowed his favorites down to a couple of dozen, and he dashed back and forth between four increasingly agitated merchants.

"Fifty pesos!" a woman shouted as Peter walked off to inspect the items on a competitor's blanket.

"Today for you, forty-five pesos," the second one shouted as the boy trotted off for another look at something farther down the sidewalk.

By the time he had made his third pass, the peddlers were shouting like buyers at a hog auction. Peter smiled broadly as one offered him a fluorescent orange frog at a price no one could refuse . . . unless they had no money. His face suddenly scrunched with concern as he remembered he was penniless, and his eyes darted back and forth atop the merchants' heads until they found me. I sighed and stood up. The show was over. It was time to visit the tourist office, which I had been dreading all morning.

The fetching smile of the English-speaking woman behind the counter melted into a sympathetic frown when I explained our problem and asked her to call the hotel. She found the place on the Internet and reluctantly dialed the number. She looked to be gripped by an intestinal malady as she relayed our request, then flinched at the reaction of the man on the other end. I heard it too: A chortle. The woman hung up the phone and switched back to English.

"They will look for the money and send it if they find it," she said without a hint of hope, but Peter heard, "Your money is on its way!"

He floated out of there on cloud nine, and his feet never touched the cobblestoned streets as we searched out a cut-rate Spanish school. Once enrolled, we set off to check out some cheap apartments, which took us again through the Zocalo.

"I'll be back in a couple of days with some money," he called to the frog peddler as he passed her blanket. "See you in a few days," he yelled to a man waving a green-and-purple cockroach. Peter was in such high spirits that I didn't have the heart to say anything. As it turned out, it didn't really matter, because within ten minutes cloud nine had bucked him off.

Oaxaca lost its charm fast as we made our way south, and so did the inhabitants. Glares replaced the tourist-area smiles, which Peter noticed long before I did. My first inkling that all was not well came when he sidled up at an intersection and put his head on my shoulder.

"Hell, Peter!" I whispered as I pushed him away. "You can't do that here."

His glistening eyes were like a knee in the gut, but what else could I have done? Two dozen people stood within a hundred feet of us, and everyone was glowering. A metalworker three shops down swung his hammer with menace, and a truck driver at the stoplight pounded his horn as if it were my deviant American face.

Working-class Mexico had long been the land of the macho man, and in 2002 he was slathered in a nasty cologne called "I Hate Gringos." The most popular chant during the country's soccer games against the US team that year was "Osama," an epithet I would later hear myself from a cackling cab driver. It was the kind of place where prudent foreigners kept their heads down, but ours were sticking up like Whack-A-Mole varmints. I'll bet those people are still talking about the day the giant American homo put the moves on his boy toy in the middle of the barrio.

I did my best to explain all this to Peter as we beat a hasty retreat. He stopped trying to hang on to me, but the way he ran one hand over the other as he scurried along in my shadow was like a caribou limping through wolf country. For the first time in a half-dozen trips south of the border, I felt like a target.

The high security walls in the barrio gave the narrow streets the feel of canals, and the traffic swept by in a honking, smoking torrent. The sidewalks were so skinny that two pedestrians could not pass without one flattening himself against the bricks, and the alternative—stepping blindly off the curb—was suicide.

Women showed their good sense by always choosing the safety of the wall, but some men seemed to view flattening as an act of submission. And while I really didn't care, I understood the implications to those who did, so whenever some tough guy tried to force me to the wall, I set my feet and made him wrestle his way past.

This was all too much for Peter, who stuck so hard to my wake that his head bounced off my back whenever I slowed. It was an exhausting way to move around, and he sighed heavily when we finally found the address we were looking for.

From the big picture window in our new apartment's kitchen, we looked down on our landlords' open courtyard and the eight-foot security wall—topped with lethal shards of broken bottles—that protected our complex. We also had a clear view of the busy street and of a ramshackle neighborhood sprawled across the flanks of a hillside to the south. Peter and I stared through the glass for several minutes after our landlords left before we migrated to the tiny living room a few feet away. I sat in an overstuffed chair, and Peter sprawled across the threadbare couch. We scanned every inch of the ceiling, walls, and floors of the little dwelling we had just committed to sharing for the next thirty days until our eyes finally met. Both sets were heavy with the same question: What now?

♥ ♥ ♥

Our apartment sat on the epicenter of pandemonium in the Western Hemisphere. The potent site was like the energy vortexes that draw new-age hippies to Sedona, Arizona, but instead of bestowing power, this one sucked it away. It must have been some kind of hell portal because if you plugged your ears and cussed you could hear the devil laughing.

The rooster next door went off at 5:20, which got a neighbor's pit bull barking. The first of a thousand daily buses chugged around the corner at six, and the honks and squealing tires of the general traffic built throughout the morning. The first pedestrians walked past our wall at about 6:30, which caused the landlords' two chows to lose their minds. The cacophony reached a crescendo at seven, when a passenger jet roared overhead so low the building shook.

Each night, propane trucks drove up and down the streets, blowing what sounded like a train whistle, and water sellers peddled bikes piled high with five-gallon jugs, singing "Aaaaaaaaaaaaaaaaaagua" until 11:00 p.m. If nothing disturbed the pit bull, I could usually get five hours of shut-eye, unless it was one of the many nights that the car alarm across the street whooped from 2:00 to 3:00 a.m.

I hardly slept that first night and was up for good with the rooster. I sat at the kitchen table in the dark, guzzling instant coffee and listening to the building bedlam as the sun rose. Peter was asleep in the next room, and every time a bus backfired or a cab laid on the horn, I expected to see his sleepy face emerge with the same "What the hell?" expression that was chiseled onto mine. But he never woke up.

I gripped the sides of the table and hung on as the jet bounced the salt shaker onto its side, then got up and peered into his room. There he lay on his lumpy bed, as peaceful as a newborn with a belly full of milk.

"Get up." I shook his bed with the heel of one foot. "Time for school."

Peter's eyes sprang open, but he didn't move. His features, so recently placid, tightened into a mask of anxiety as the import of those last three words hit home. He was going to have to go back out *there*.

"I don't feel so good," he said, clutching his stomach dramatically. "Maybe I ought to stay home today."

"Get up," I repeated, stifling a yawn. I grabbed his hand, and as I pulled him to his feet, his other hand yanked the sheet from the bed. He held it in front of him in a vain attempt to hide the fact that he was stark freakin' naked.

"Where are your clothes?" I demanded, and he nodded toward a pile in the corner.

"They're all dirty," he said. "Maybe I can do some laundry while you're at school."

"No way. Just take a quick shower and put on whatever's cleanest. We can do some laundry later."

He trudged off and joined me in the kitchen a few minutes later.

"Why do I have to learn Spanish anyway?" A note of panic had crept into his voice. "I ought to stay here and work on my real schoolwork."

I rolled my eyes. The kid was a C-student, and I suspected that he was given a D in algebra the previous term only so the school didn't have to make him repeat seventh grade.

"There will be plenty of time for homework later, Aristotle. Now eat your cereal, and let's get out of here."

Five minutes later we were back outside for another half hour of Sidewalk Chicken. We weren't halfway up the block before we met our first contestant, a white-haired man in neat black slacks and a white dress shirt. He presented a dilemma because while he was obviously in a more genteel class than the workmen with whom I'd collided the day before, he was also barreling down the sidewalk with the same get-out-of-my-way aggressiveness. I slowed to assess the situation, and Peter drilled my scapula with the crown of his skull.

"Will you watch—" I began but never finished. When I turned my head to yell, the old guy slipped alongside, dipped his shoulder, and nudged me off the curb. I hopped back onto the sidewalk like a cricket from a frying pan and watched the wily fox slide past Peter with nary a backward glance.

Celebrating apparently was not allowed in this screwed-up game. In fact, keeping minor collisions from escalating into something serious seemed to require that both sides maintain the fiction that there had been no contact at all.

Fine. I could do that. When I spotted our next contestant, a high-school punk who had separated from a group at the corner to nonchalantly block my way, I leaned forward and called out, "Stay close, Peter, and don't look back."

I heard the air explode from the surprised teen's lungs as we hit, and I fought the urge to stare as he spun off somewhere to my right. An angry buzz erupted from the pack, which told me I might have put a little too much oomph into it, but no one came after us, so I guessed I had stayed within bounds.

Peter was traumatized. We had a twenty-minute break halfway through our four-hour classes, but he refused to leave the building when I dashed around the corner to buy a cold drink.

On the walk home he stuck so close to my wake that my slightest hesitation sent him careening off the nape of my neck. This caused some confusion when my attempts to be polite—"Perdón, señora," for example—were immediately followed by a string of English cusswords.

He slumped against the wall when I finally turned the lock on the security door. Then he led the way up the two flights of stairs to our apartment and collapsed on the couch. He lay there with one forearm across his eyes like some old matron with the vapors, and I knew that if things didn't change soon, he'd wind up with ulcers and a nervous tic. I also knew I had no idea what to do about it.

SIX

A towering thunderstorm barreled in from the west and cooled our apartment down to a pleasant seventy degrees. Peter dozed on the couch while I stood in the breeze by the window and watched the runoff carry heaps of trash down the street. I moved to the overstuffed chair after a while and watched the boy sleep, but I was up in less than a minute and back at the window. We'd been sitting around the apartment or in class for days now and had sat all day in the car for most of the previous week. I wanted to go out and find a track to run some sprints, but I knew the very idea would give the kid a conniption. I moved back to the living room and slumped into the chair.

Peter reminded me a lot of myself at age thirteen. I had been big and gangly and socially awkward, and I wasn't exactly brimming with self-esteem. Always the new kid as we moved to seven states in seven years, I also knew what it felt like to be picked on. Somewhere along the way, however, I had decided to do something about it. Like the proverbial skinny boy who gets sand kicked in his face, I became hell-bent on exercising my way to a frame imposing enough to keep bullies at bay.

Good luck with that at age thirteen. I was still a beanpole a few months after I started my regimen, but I had gained something more important than muscle. Like the five-foot-one housewife who shouldered me out of her path as she exited her first kickboxing class a couple of decades later, I *felt* tougher. Though I was still no more capable a fighter than all those years when I'd been socked in the nose or tripped on the playground, the bullies were no longer so sure about it. From then on they searched for easier prey.

Peter, however, had always been completely uninterested in exercise. The example I'd set with daily workouts had provided no inspiration, and neither had the twenty-five cents per pull-up I'd offered as a weekly incentive. He just didn't like to break a sweat, and like any normal kid, he had resisted his parents' effort to push him into it.

There in the south of Mexico, however, I decided give it one last try. As I sat there staring, I was struck with the overwhelming certitude that more strength would give him the confidence he needed to survive, if not enjoy, the rest of the trip.

But how could I get Peter to understand? I could try reasoning with him, telling him my skinny-boy story, but he didn't want my advice. Who was I to give advice anyway after ignoring him for so long?

I watched him doze as I pondered the problem for the next ten minutes. I finally came to grips with the fact that I just didn't have the sensitivity to pull off a conversation on a delicate topic like a boy's self-esteem. I had to go with what I had. I whipped a pillow across the room and caught him full on the side of the head.

"You have a better chance of spotting Bigfoot than of ever seeing your money belt again," I hollered as his startled eyes flew open. "That cash is gone forever."

His head snapped back as if he'd been slapped, and I jumped up to race to my room. He was on the verge of tears when I returned twenty seconds later, but his eyes sparkled with interest when he saw what I was carrying.

"What's that for?" he asked as I began laying hundred-peso bills on the kitchen table.

"This is a hundred dollars. That's about what you had in your money belt, right?"

"Yeah!" He gazed with the longing of a hungry mutt at a T-bone steak, and I knew I had him.

"I have a little deal for you: Exercise whenever I do, as hard as I do, and for as long as I do, and I'll give you this money."

If he was disappointed in the attached string, he didn't show it. I held out my hand, and he shook it with a smile. Then he scooped up the cash and disappeared into his bedroom. When he returned, he was still grinning.

"How about some burritos?" he asked. "I'll buy if you fly."

"Maybe later," I said, slowing leaning forward until I was touching my toes. "But we probably ought to see how we feel after our workout."

Peter's smile faded. "What? Now?"

We dropped to the floor and pounded out a set of push-ups. Peter flipped onto his back after his twelfth, gasped like an old man having a heart attack, rolled to his knees, and crawled onto the couch.

"Good workout," he wheezed. He stretched his arms far over his head and yawned. He seemed to be preparing for a nap.

I jogged to the front door and waved for him to follow. He frowned with concern. I led him onto the landing and down the first three steps of the open metal staircase, and his frown deepened. When I reached out and grabbed the step above my head, I could hear a little moan of recognition.

Pull-ups!

Then it was inside again for sit-ups, after which Peter crawled back onto the couch.

"What are you doing?" he asked nervously as I paced in front of him, staring at my watch.

"Counting down the seconds. Ready?"

"For what?"

"Your next set of push-ups. We're doing four of everything."

He rolled to the floor and glared as he positioned his hands.

"You can buy your own burrito," he said, then slid his feet back and eased his skinny chest to the floor.

♥ ♥ ♥

Whether because of the exercise or the repetition of our forays into the street during the next few days, Peter began to calm down. He still stayed close on our walks, but he stopped bouncing off my back when I stopped. I can't say he was enjoying the Oaxaca experience, however.

Our days began at 6:30 a.m. with lukewarm showers. A cornflake breakfast awaited us at seven, followed by a half-hour walk to school. At noon we dodged our way home, fixed lunch, studied, exercised, cleaned, shopped in the market, cooked, ate, and did dishes. We never had time for much else during the school week because everything took so long. What was a simple task in Salt Lake City—popping a plate of leftovers into the microwave or a load of laundry into the washer—was an hours-long challenge in Mexico.

The on-site laundry facilities consisted of a washboard and two buckets on the apartment's flat roof. Whoever worked the washboard always rasped the skin off a knuckle, and Peter seemed to take it personally. *Some adventure,* his eyes complained as he kneaded a pair of pants in a bucket. *We could have saved a lot of trouble by just staying home and hiring on as maids.*

The only time I can remember Peter looking as though he was enjoying himself was when he was sleeping, and for the first week he was able to do

it for a solid ten hours a night. But then Oaxaca entered its festival season, and the boy met his match. Sleep was measured in one- or two-hour spurts between the flying bombs that revelers launched all night to honor their church's patron saint. We were jarred awake at 1:00 a.m. one morning by a rapid series of blasts so close I thought we were being shelled. In between explosions, the ringing in my ears sounded like a bad brass band, and it took a few minutes to realize there really was one playing somewhere in the distance.

We left our rooms at the same time and staggered to the kitchen window. In the courtyard below, the landlords were trying to calm their dogs, Kit and Winnie.

Winnie was a pretty, black male who would bark and turn circles whenever we came downstairs. Kit didn't move much except for an ugly head that bobbed continually as it swung slowly back and forth. He was blind and half deaf, nearly bald, and reeked like the accidents he lay in all day. He was fifteen going on dead and looked like roadkill that had been forgotten in the rain.

"Buenos días," Peter called, and our landlords gestured for us to come down. Pinar and Alberto lived on the outskirts of Oaxaca, but they ran their accounting business out of rooms on the first floor of our building and often slept there during the week. When we got downstairs, I could see they were getting ready to go out.

"It is the festival for the church," Pinar said, as excited as a little girl on Christmas Eve. "You must come with us."

So we walked off into the night in an area that had a menacing air during the day, trusting that our landlords knew what they were doing. As we followed the couple up one dark street and down another, the music grew progressively louder. Finally we turned up an alley that reverberated with the *blat*s and *oompah*s of poorly played horns. People in the street beyond danced in the headlights of an unseen vehicle.

We stepped out of the alley into a fever dream of cowboys and princesses and ten-foot-tall papier-mâché freaks. Hundreds of people of all ages were dancing in and out of shadows around floats carrying lambs and Jesus statues and little girls in sparkling crowns—all propelled by battered pickups filled with drunken men in denim jackets and cowboy hats.

An old man thrust a cup into my hand, filled it with rotgut moonshine from a plastic jug, and topped it off while I was still choking from the first sip. A middle-aged woman handed me a slice of buttered toast and blew hot tequila breath in my ear as she slurred something I couldn't understand.

Everyone was smiling, and their happiness was contagious. Peter was laughing with our landlords at the bizarre expressions on the giant masks. I was knocking back the moonshine and exchanging handshakes and backslaps with men with whom I'd been trading hard looks for days.

When we got back to the apartment, we stood by the kitchen window for half an hour, Peter chattering nonstop about all he had seen, and me wondering whether I could throw something far enough to wallop the car that was whooping it up for the third time that week. And suddenly it was back, that connection we'd shared during our first hour on the road when everything still seemed possible. We grinned and giggled and poked and pushed, united by an unexpected affection for our formerly scary neighbors in the barrio.

Or most of them, anyway. When Peter went to bed, I crept up onto the roof with a bag of grapefruit and an arm that felt like Tom Brady's. The whooping car never shut up that night, but I still slept a lot more peacefully.

♥ ♥ ♥

With everything else taking so much time, it seemed natural to Peter to cut back on the only thing he controlled: homework. I was still on my first page of Spanish assignments the next afternoon when Peter closed his notebook with a slap and got up from the table.

"Hey! What about your algebra?" I snapped, and he moped back over and hen-scratched his way through a chapter in about twenty minutes.

I smelled a rat. If the kid were capable of solving fifteen math problems in the time it took to scribble them, he wouldn't have gotten a D last term. For the first time in years, I sat down to check his work, and my initial challenge was deciphering the hieroglyphics.

"What's this number?" I asked, pointing to what looked like a seven but could as easily have been a nine.

"I think that's a B," he said.

I checked the answer in the back of the book, and Peter's was wrong.

"What's this number here?"

"Uhhhhh, a three? No, it's, uhhhhh . . ."

We checked the answer, and enough of his legible numbers were wrong that I moved on to the next problem.

I fought my way through eight of them, each of which had been criminally butchered, before I pushed away from the table.

"I want my hundred bucks back," I bellowed. "You're going home!"

I was already going to catch enough hell for this trip once everyone figured out what the big rush to get out of town had really been about. If Peter came back half a year behind his class, I would have no cover whatsoever.

He stared back in horror, which took me by surprise. As hard as the trip had been thus far, I had half expected him to jump up and start packing. But he was frozen in place, afraid to blink or even breathe. I began to waver. After all, he had put in the same effort as he always had; the only difference this time was that I had taken an interest in the product. It wouldn't be fair to send him home without another chance.

I took a deep breath and started over. "Look, Peter, I promised everyone this trip would be good for you. You can't go home worse than you left. You have to go home better."

His breath came out in a rush. "I will. I mean I am. I can already do twenty-five push-ups." His eyes were wide, pleading.

"I know about the push-ups," I said. "I'm talking about the schoolwork."

I slid his books across a few inches of table until they were directly in front of him.

"Here's the deal. I'm going to give you another chance. But the next time I find even *one* wrong answer or misspelled word, you will be on the next flight home."

He slumped against the chair, weak with relief. Then he held out a trembling hand for me to shake before picking up his pencil with clear resolve. He spent the next hour and a half fixing, checking, and rechecking his math. He spent another half hour correcting his Spanish. When he finished, he stood up from the table and called me over.

"It's perfect. Check it."

I was lying on the couch reading a book, but instead of getting up, I just shook my head. "I believe you," I said, as if I had a choice. If I had checked his work and found an error I would have had to send him home, and with the effort he had just shown, I was not ready to do that. I figured the hard work alone should earn him a few more days regardless of his answers. I promised myself I would check his assignments next week.

I expected a whoop of relief, but Peter didn't move. He stood there with a crooked smile, and after a few seconds his eyes began to glisten.

"What's wrong?" I asked, and as I sat up he wiped the heels of his hands across his cheekbones.

"Nothing," he said. He stared at the floor, still sporting that funny smile. "It's just that you don't ever usually believe me." He looked up quickly, afraid he might have crossed a line, and his smile faded. "Dad?"

I must have been looking pretty funny myself. A truth so big and awful will do that to a person. For the first time in years, I'd seen a flash of pride in Peter's eyes, and the catalyst had been three simple words from me: "I believe you."

What a wonderful yet miserable epiphany! I'd stumbled across the root of my son's low self-esteem, but the fact that it was me put a big, soggy damper on the discovery.

"Come here," I said quietly, and I made some room on the couch. I had to say something, but for half a minute I couldn't think of what. Finally, I took a deep breath and gave the truth a try.

"I know I can be a jerk," I began, and I nearly proved it when Peter started nodding his head enthusiastically. I took another breath and moved on. "I just need you to know that it's not your fault. It never has been. I'm proud of you, even if I don't always show it."

We sat in silence for a few more seconds before I reached into my pocket, pulled out a ten-peso coin, and dropped it in his lap. And with that we struck the most important bargain of all: If I ever said something unfriendly I would pay him a fine, the amount determined by the severity of the infraction. Lobbing an F-bomb, for example, would cost me fifty pesos. Raising my voice would cost me five. I was going to be a considerate person, by God, or go broke in the attempt.

"Well, that's my plan," I added. "What do you think?"

Peter sat quietly for a few seconds before a smile slowly spread across his face.

"I think I'm going to be rich."

SEVEN

I woke up the morning after Mexico's Independence Day with a pounding headache and a hallucination that made me swear off bootleg mescal. I'd made a mistake by not going to bed when Peter did. Instead, I'd snuck up onto the roof with a bottle to stand in solidarity with my Mexican hermanos until the shelling died down enough to sleep.

This time I gave myself brain damage, I thought as I rubbed my temples and watched Kate Moss's anorexic brother flex like Mr. America in my living room.

Our apartment was built from converted office space, and the wall between my bedroom and the rest of our apartment was a floor-to-ceiling sheet of glass. When I looked again I realized I wasn't delirious, but the reality still made me do a double take. After only two weeks of workouts, Peter stood in front of the mirror in his boxers, running his fingers approvingly over new faint lines in his abdomen, shoulders, triceps, and biceps.

While the calisthenics had not put much meat on his bony frame, he had carved enough definition to see what muscle he had. He turned to the side and pulled himself into a posture that would have warmed a drill sergeant's heart before continuing on to the shower.

A pat on the back for the old man, I thought as I sat up in bed, but I quickly lost that lovin' feeling. My stomach was rolling.

Peter was out of the shower before I even left my room, which told me that the hot water was off again. That meant my shower would take twice as long because if I walked into a cold stream that morning, my head would blow right off my neck. The best I could manage was to stand to the side and splash one small area at a time. When I finally walked into the kitchen, Peter was dressed and rummaging in the cupboard under the sink.

"Where's the grapefruit?" he asked, and my left hand unconsciously moved to my throwing arm, which was a little tender this morning. As he stood up, I struggled to keep my eyes on his face instead of drifting to the disturbing scene through the window behind him. It looked as though the whooping car had been caught in another citrus storm. Leathery yellow peels—torn to pieces by the murderous impact—littered the surrounding street and sidewalk; pink, sticky pulp was strewn upon the hood, roof, and windshield.

"Sheesh, I dunno, we're really going through those things fast," I said quickly as I backed away toward my room. "Just have some cereal. We'll get more fruit at the market later."

I pulled on some clothes and wobbled after him down the metal staircase to the concrete courtyard. We gave the dogs a pat on the way past and stepped through the doorway onto the sidewalk. I kept my eyes focused up the street and set off fast enough to make sure Peter wouldn't pause to look around. I saw no upside in him learning that his dad was a serial fruit bomber, especially since my only defense was that I drank too much moonshine.

I slowed as we turned down a side street, but he hadn't noticed my erratic pace. He was too excited about the day's activity. In the guidebook, he had found a town famous for producing stainless-steel blades, and he was hoping to get a good deal on a guillotine.

We strolled toward the second-class bus station on mostly empty sidewalks, hemmed on both sides by the town's ubiquitous security walls. Traffic was light this Sunday morning, though the few cars raced past so fast that they made as much noise as the regular weekday flow. Dogs took their lives in their paws as they trotted from one sidewalk to the other because it was not in the local drivers' DNA to slow down. In fact, some sped up and veered wildly in an effort to hit the strays. As a cab barreled straight for us in an attempt to murder a crossing dog, Peter and I threw ourselves against the wall and braced for the ugly impact. But the driver swerved at the last second as the mutt nonchalantly hopped the curb. A wily veteran of such crossings, it had never altered its stride.

I waved Peter ahead since so few people were out, and though he looked a little sickly as he slid to the front, I immediately spotted a difference. Instead of hunching over in an attempt to become invisible as he had for the past two weeks, he stood up straighter. The hands that he had always kept laced in front of him when he walked now hung from arms that swung in rhythm with his steps, albeit as stiffly as a rusty robot's.

He had also developed his own rules for Sidewalk Chicken. When he saw trouble coming, he glanced behind him and adjusted his speed to meet the other guy during a break in traffic. Instead of flattening against the wall he stepped briefly off the curb. I was concerned at first, but he became such a master of the tactic that he not only didn't let a car get near him, he never even had to break stride. That caused more than one guy to lose his balance after leaning in for a collision that never came.

He led us through a gate to a dirt lot on which a couple of buses stood idling. One was a battered, gray tourist carrier, which marked it as a second-class ride with reserved seating. The other, an old American school bus, was the kind of third-class free-for-all we always tried to avoid. There was no rider limit on those, and the last time we took one we had shared a child-size seat with two adults, one of whom was lugging a dead pig and four thousand flies.

I bought two second-class tickets at a plywood booth and nodded at the gray bus with raised eyebrows. The attendant pursed his lips and shook his head. "Sit there," he said, pointing to a bench a few feet away.

We took our seats, and Peter immediately leaned across his knees for a better look at something on the sandy ground.

"Hey, leaf-cutter ants!" he announced, to which I responded with a hearty "Bulls—!"

I tossed a ten-peso coin at his feet and bent down to sort things out, but the kid was right. A big line of the crafty insects ran past the bench to a hole in the cinder-block wall, and each one was carrying a scrap of leaf about three times its size. I'd been so excited to see leaf-cutters in the Costa Rican jungle in the early '90s that it had almost made up for the preposterous cost of getting there, and now I found out that they were a common Mexican pest.

"Son of a . . ." I began, but I caught myself as Peter's smirking face turned my way. The fines had become a joke, with him holding out his hand for payment a lot of times before I even finished cussing. But he hadn't made as much money as he thought he would because slowly but surely I was getting a handle on my mouth.

I had a good test ten minutes later when I strolled back to the ticket booth.

"When does the bus leave for Ejutla?" I asked.

"It left," the attendant replied. Two men nearby nodded their heads in agreement. "It was the gray one," he added.

"But you told us not to get on that bus," I said incredulously, and the attendant looked concerned. There had obviously been some misunderstanding. He had probably meant that we could not board the bus at that instant, but he assumed we knew we could get on when everyone else queued up.

Why he had let us sit there while the bus drove off was something I couldn't fathom, but now he was queasy with regret. He yelled something to a man standing near the school bus, which was already loaded and about to pull away. That man shouted something to the driver, who climbed out of the bus and walked over to the booth, clearly irritated. The attendant and the driver argued back and forth for a minute before the driver stormed back to his vehicle.

"You can go with him," the attendant said.

We followed the driver aboard the bus and immediately understood why he hadn't wanted us along. Even the aisles were packed with people. He yelled and shoved until the line contracted enough to give us a place to stand. Each seat was jammed so full that even though I stood sideways my thighs were squeezed between both outside riders. Being a few inches shorter, Peter had it worse. The shoulder of one passenger speared his butt while another's was jammed into his groin.

That's how we traveled for the next hour, so even when a back wheel fell off and the bus fishtailed into the weeds, the emotion that overwhelmed all others was relief that the ride was over. Peter and I hobbled off and watched at least a hundred stoic locals disembark. Most piled baskets on their heads and set off up the weed-lined road without so much as a glance at the naked axle, as if this kind of thing happened all the time.

We followed the line of refugees into Ejutla, a pleasant little town with a big, shady park but not a single maker of blades large or small. We walked up one street and down another, stopping everyone we saw, but no one had ever heard of a fancy knife or sword being sold in Ejutla, much less fashioned there.

We walked back to the edge of town and waited in another line until the bus to Oaxaca arrived. Not a word was spoken by anyone during the hour we stood there. The only occurrence worth noting was that the man in front of me unzipped his fly and peed on the weeds. No one, not even a woman whom he bumped again and again as he swayed hypnotically with both hands on his privates, paid him the least bit of attention.

● ● ●

Our recreational fiasco to Ejutla was not a total loss. From that day on we had a versatile word to describe money wasted or time badly spent. We pronounced it *A-hoot-lah*.

We were Ahootlahed the night we blew five bucks to enter a sports bar, expecting to see the University of Utah play football on ESPN, only to discover that Latin America has its own soccer-heavy version of the network. Our detour through Mexico City had been Ahootlah-squared, and Peter even hurled the word as an epithet.

"This car is a money-sucking Ahootlah," he muttered one afternoon as we walked through the parking lot where we were storing the Dart for the month. The right rear tire was going bald, so we decided to go ahead and replace it that day as well as get a long-overdue oil change. Peter chattered with the guard for a few seconds before directing us down the street to a mechanic's yard.

His language skills were threatening to leave mine in the dust. Even though my two years of college Spanish gave me a more thorough understanding of the grammar—for the time being—his ear was better, and he learned ten times faster. My only clear advantage was my accent. According to the teachers at our school, I spoke exactly like a college-bound Spaniard. If only people hadn't insisted on answering.

At the yard I hopped out and issued instructions in such beautiful Castilian that I had to lace my fingers to keep from patting myself on the back. Then the mechanic ruined the moment by firing hundred-mile-per-hour Spanish at my ten-mile-per-hour ear, and all I could do was smile and nod.

From our seat on the trunk of a junk car, Peter and I watched the man pull the Dart under a tin-roofed lean-to about thirty feet away. Lord only knew what I had agreed to, so I studied him closely. He made quick work of the tire change, and when he popped the hood I strolled over just to make sure things were going as planned.

"You are changing the oil now?" I asked the mechanic, and he nodded with a friendly smile.

I strutted back to my seat with my inner Mexican doing the cha-cha. I may not have understood a word he said, but he had obviously understood me just fine. I silently practiced an elaborate speech of gracious gratitude to bestow upon the man when he was done, and I even threw a little of the lingo at Peter.

"The mechanic changed the tire and will soon be done with the oil," I announced proudly. It's always nice when you can demonstrate competence in front of your son, and I had just knocked the ball out of the park. "He is almost finished."

"No he's not," Peter replied immediately with an accent crisper than mine. "He still has to clean the engine."

I dropped the Spanish. "He's not going to clean the engine," I said defensively.

"Uh-huh. You told him to."

"I never told him to do that," I insisted, but I was starting to sweat.

"Well," Peter announced finally, "you said yes." He nodded toward the car, which had disappeared in a cloud of steam so colossal that it completely consumed the mechanic's little work bay.

I won't repeat what I said next, but it earned Peter a quick fifty pesos. I sprinted to the car and stopped the cleaning, but it was too late. All the engine components were soaked, and as I watched the water drip into the open coils of the alternator, I knew it was Ahootlahed. It would fester in the tropical climate until it rusted and seized; it was only a matter of time. I didn't bother reciting my speech when the mechanic handed me the keys. I just smiled weakly and drove back to the parking lot.

❤ ❤ ❤

The Internet café near the Zocalo was always packed with well-dressed Mexican kids, which made me aware of how ratty all the tourists appeared. We must have read the same guidebook advice about "blending in" with the natives, but even in the poor neighborhoods, Mexicans' clothes were in better shape than ours. The only people we could blend with were beggars.

Ah, well, better to look poor than affluent in Latin America, I always said, but Peter didn't share my opinion. He carried his BMW key chain everywhere as a talisman against his temporary poverty, and he spent fifty-eight minutes of any hour on the Internet cruising sites featuring expensive cars, clothes, and ski equipment. He would then spend the next half hour telling me about the tailored suit or designer sunglasses he was thinking of acquiring and the next ten minutes trying to finagle more money out of me.

"What if I do twice as many push-ups? Can I have another hundred dollars?"

"No."

"What if I do more sit-ups?"

"No."

"Please?"

"No."

"What if I do more pull-ups?"

"No."

"Please?"

"No."

"What if I just drop this water jug on the floor and make you cuss?"

"What if I drop you out the window?"

"That's a threat! You owe me fifty pesos!"

The kid was relentless. I finally paid him twenty pesos to knock it off for twenty-four hours, but it didn't stop his wheels from turning. We reached the running track exactly twenty-three hours and fifty-one minutes later, and halfway down the backstretch on our third three-hundred-meter dash, Peter yelled, "Please?"

And that wasn't the end of it. He hectored me between gasps for breath as we rested the three minutes until our next run, and I no longer felt half as guilty about having suppressed his chatter back home. Heck, the fact that I hadn't maimed him demonstrated a capacity for patience well beyond that of the average man.

But when he abruptly fell silent, I wasn't happy. A chorus of whistles and catcalls had erupted from the nearby bleachers, punctuated by enough *gringos* to leave no doubt about the target. Peter looked tense. Our eyes briefly met before I turned to face the bleachers, and the half-dozen men drinking beer high in the stands stopped their whooping and looked away, though I could see they were still snickering.

All talk, I thought, and more of it flew the moment I turned around. Had the men stood in open challenge when I'd faced them I'd have led Peter off the track at a fast trot, but a few boozy insults wouldn't hurt anybody. I tapped Peter's shoulder and walked back to the line for another run.

We started at the end of the curve on the side farthest from the bleachers, which meant our final hundred meters ran directly in front of them. The men exploded in jeers every time we passed.

Peter attacked each run with grim resolve, and I assumed he wanted nothing more than to get the workout over with and go home. So he caught me off guard when he challenged me to a race as we walked up to the line for our final sprint.

"Give me twenty bucks if I win," he added.

"Ten," I answered reflexively, though I'm not sure why I bothered. The figure could have been ten or ten thousand. The kid had only been training for about three weeks. It wasn't as if he had a chance of winning.

But the next thing I knew I was staring at his skinny back, and he was pulling away! As I chased him down the first hundred meters, I had flashbacks to our prior four runs. I couldn't believe it hadn't registered that after pushing the pace at the top of every final stretch Peter had abruptly geared down, leaving me to spend my reserves on a full-tilt dash to the finish. And the little sandbagger had devised and carried out his treacherous scheme amid the cacophony of taunts that had kept me hopelessly distracted!

Righteous indignation powered my legs into the curve, and when I caught him on the far side I figured the race was over. But annoyance turned to panic as Peter began to surge ahead again. For a few awful seconds, I thought I was going to have to trip him, but he eased up as we came into the final straight. I swiveled my head and grinned as I drew even, but he wasn't looking at me. The jeering section had left their seats and hotfooted it down the bleacher stairs to the track, across which they were now sauntering at a pace clearly intended to impede. They went single-file, eyes ahead, pantomiming ignorance of the two foreigners who were barreling in from forty meters . . . thirty meters . . . twenty meters away.

It was a variation of Sidewalk Chicken with the same macho motivation. If the men forced us to slow or veer from the lanes that were unmistakably ours, they would win. We would lose any respect they had for us, which, though miniscule, had at least been sufficient to keep them from doing more than lobbing insults.

I held my course and velocity, but Peter sprang ahead. He had gauged everyone's pace and determined that with a little more juice he could pass unscathed through a break in the line, which he did a foot ahead of one of the men. I passed through the same hole, though by the time I got there I had to widen it a little with a lowered shoulder. I continued down the track as if I hadn't noticed the collision, which apparently appeased the men because they didn't come after us. I had, after all, played by their passive-aggressive rules.

Peter was energized. He had won a race and ten dollars, and he thought he might be able to hustle a few more bucks on the basketball court. But I just wanted to go home. I was exhausted and sore, having pulled something in my thigh in a last, desperate push to catch him at the finish.

He circled me like a gnat, leaning in close to poke my ribs and dodging away before I could get my hands around his scrawny neck.

"What's wrong, old man? Can't move?" He danced close and poked me again.

Old man, huh? Okay, you little . . .

I hobbled over to the corner of the bleachers, tweaked my back with an awkward crouch to pick up the basketball, and led the way at a fast limp across the track to the asphalt courts.

We always started a basketball session by running the same warm-up drill, and though we were already plenty warm, we did it out of habit. I held the ball at the top of the key while Peter ran from the baseline to the free-throw line. I tossed him the ball, and as I sprinted past he flipped it back to me and drifted out to my former spot. I dribbled to the baseline and whipped the ball back to Peter, who stepped forward and shot a jumper.

We had been repeating the drill for a few minutes when I noticed four men walking toward us across an adjoining soccer field. It was some of the guys from the bleachers, heading back from the store with fresh quart bottles of beer. They stopped at the side of the court and watched us shoot free throws as if they were waiting for a game, but they weren't dressed for one. They wore long pants, cuffed shirts, work boots, and scowls, and they just stared in response to my friendly nod. I was thinking it might be a good time to call it a day when the men set down their bottles and moved forward.

"Let's play," said a heavyset young guy with a thick black mustache, though there was nothing playful about his tone.

"We were just leav—" I began, but Peter tossed the guy the ball. I hit the kid with some serious stink-eye as the men lined up to shoot free-throws for teams. He didn't even really like the freakin' game. What was he thinking?

Mustache-man missed a free throw, stepped aside, and waved me to the line. I made the shot, as did Peter, and then we watched as the other men took turns missing for the next minute. Finally, a shot went in, and the teams were set.

If there were a graph showing the state of US–Mexico relations in September 2002, that game would have knocked the arrow down a couple of lines. Mustache-man picked up the ball at the top of the key, ran like an NFL fullback, and kneed me in the groin. I clubbed his head with an elbow as I blocked his shot, and we wound up in a heap on the asphalt.

Every time Peter touched the ball he was smacked, knocked down, or kicked, and I came close to dropping the pretense and taking an honest swing at the SOBs. But the kid was fighting his own battles. His arms were scratched and bruised, and he was bleeding from a cut on his forehead, but he wasn't looking to me for help, and he wasn't backing down. He was even getting in his own cheap shots whenever he got a chance, so I stayed out of it and concentrated on keeping my man from gouging my eyes.

The role of the Mexican on our team turned out to be letting his buddy score at will, so we found ourselves tied at ten in a game to eleven.

I caught Peter's attention.

"Run the drill," I mouthed, and he gave a little nod before walking to his spot. I took the ball at the top of the key, faked a pass to our Mexican teammate, and tossed it to Peter, who took such a ferocious elbow in the back upon stopping at the free-throw line that he sprawled across the blacktop. He flipped me the ball as he went down, though, and as I drove toward the baseline both Mustache-man and Peter's guy followed. When I leapt and threw the ball back to Peter, he was alone. He took one dribble, rose up, and fired the winning shot just as a late-arriving defender flattened him again with a forearm to the stomach.

Peter got up, brushed himself off, and hobbled over to pick up the ball, which had rolled a few feet onto the soccer field beyond the basket. The men sauntered back to their bottles and walked off toward the bleachers without a word.

Peter watched them go as he limped back with the ball, flipped it through the hoop, caught it, and led the way calmly off the court. His shoulders stayed soldier-square as we made our way through the city to our apartment, which I know because he was in front of me the whole time. And I'm not sure whether it was his defiant posture, the blood on his resolute face, or a combination of the two, but no one tried to force him to the wall on the long walk home.

EIGHT

Viewed from the lumpy perch of our threadbare couch, our modest apartment was a cheery place. With the tropical sun beating through the kitchen's picture window, a canary-yellow light seemed to radiate from the plaster walls. The chrome handles on our black-and-white mini-stove sparkled in relief, and the red squares on our checkered tablecloth glowed like embers in a campfire.

The light show abruptly ended when the clouds moved in for the afternoon rains, but the accompanying breeze—at least twenty degrees cooler—more than made up for the gloom. I would have gladly hunkered down there for a second month, but Peter was eager to resume our journey south. So eager, in fact, that he had spent an afternoon on the Internet researching Central American towns with Spanish schools.

Impressed with his initiative, I smiled as I sat down to review his report. It was a comprehensive list featuring restaurant prices as well as lodging options offered by the various schools. When I finished reading I had only one question:

"Are you so strapped for cash that you're *trying* to make me cuss?"

Peter had highlighted ten schools, all on the beach and all of which offered additional scuba packages. The cheapest was 250 dollars a week per person, and it didn't include room and board.

"But we can get rice and beans near that one for two bucks," Peter implored. "Think of what we'll save on food!"

"They could pay *us* two bucks a meal and we'd still go broke," I groused as I got up to retrieve the Central America guidebook. We spent the next hour looking up cheaper options before settling on Quetzaltenango, Guatemala. It was a fair-sized city in the western highlands with at least a dozen cheap language schools, and the prices for food and lodging were about half of those in Mexico. Peter was disappointed to be so far from the beach, but the savings reaped in Guatemala would keep his scuba dreams afloat for another month.

Alberto and Pinar fixed us breakfast in the courtyard the next morning while we awaited the cab that would haul our luggage to the Dart. The bags sat piled against the security wall at least fifteen feet from Winnie, who nonetheless made a valiant attempt to splash them with whiz from the far limit of his chain. Even more than our kindhearted landlords, we were going to miss the foul animal, who never failed to greet us as if we were long-lost family. Kit had been declared officially dead a few days before, and while I was never clear about what had tipped off his owners, they were devastated.

"Ah, Kit, Kit, Kit," Alberto whispered as he stared at the stained patch of concrete where the dog had lain for years. "Ahhhhh, Kit," Pinar sighed, dusting her bangs with tortilla crumbs as she wiped her eye. After a few more minutes they couldn't take it anymore. They abruptly stood up, wished us a safe journey, and disappeared into their apartment.

As I finished my breakfast and watched to make sure Winnie's stream pooled short of our bags, I had an unsettling feeling that I didn't fully process until we stepped from the cab and began piling our belongings next to the Dart. Somehow, despite the aggravation caused by bringing so much stuff from Salt Lake, we had accumulated even more in Oaxaca. When we drove out of town I could see nothing but bags in my rearview mirror.

Adding insult to injury, from somewhere deep in the pile of flotsam rose a stench so rancid that even the wind blowing through the open windows couldn't hold it back.

"Did you . . . ?" I began, but it was clear from the disgust on Peter's face that he was about to accuse me. So we pulled off the road in Santa María de Tule and unloaded everything onto the roof and trunk.

Peter unzipped a duffel and peered inside.

"Kit? Is that you, boy?"

He gave the contents a quick whiff, zipped it up, and tossed it back into the car. We repeated the process until the back seat was again packed to the ceiling, but we never found the source of the odor. I figured we must have hit a leprous rat or some other sick varmint on the way out of Oaxaca, and it would take a few dozen miles to shake the remnants from the axles.

We had bigger problems at the moment, however, because we faced the daunting task of backing up blindly into a bumper-to-bumper traffic stream that never seemed to ebb. Every time I rolled an inch I provoked a riot of horns and shouts, which finally caught the attention of a local policeman. He asked for a "donation to the church" before walking into the road and stopping traffic, and I began to remember why we had so disliked that first week on the road. The town's mammoth topes also jarred my memory, along with my molars, and south of town we hit potholes so deep the steering started pulling. When I saw the first Pemex station and noted that gas prices had risen to more than two sixty a gallon, I tossed a wad of pesos on the seat.

"Don't take this personally," I said, "but I have a feeling you are on the verge of earning some serious cash."

We drove all day through a bewitching mix of desert and tropical greenery. Stands of grand palms waved in the shadows of cacti the size of townhouses, but I had a hard time appreciating the scenery, distracted as I was by a vision of border gangs having a Black Friday free-for-all in my back seat. The banshee in the tailpipe screamed *Iiiiiiiiiiiidiot!* at every tope, and all I could do was whisper, "You got that right."

I also couldn't stop my mind from drifting toward my future back home. I didn't think I could face starting over on the bottom rung of the ladder, but what else was I going to do? At times, if I began with the proposition that I hailed from the land of opportunity, I could answer the question with confidence if not specificity. The possibilities were endless even if I couldn't seem to put my finger on one. But the longer I pondered the question, the more agitated I became. The vultures that had earlier gamboled on distant updrafts began appearing on nearby fence posts, as if drawn by the scent of my growing panic.

Peter lay low all day and pocketed whatever cash came his way. At first he watched me stew with a mixture of disappointment and avarice, but it wasn't long before the balmy heat and the maritime sway of the big sedan caused his eyelids to droop. He'd been curled up against the door for an hour when we came upon a horseman who was letting his sweaty steed dance on and off the highway at will, and I let loose a low stream of vile profanity that I thought was inaudible above the wind. But Peter's left hand slipped from his lap like the head of some sightless bird, pecked at the seat until it encountered a crumpled bill, and fed it to his pocket before crawling back into his lap. He never even opened an eye.

I know he was sleeping for the two hours prior to our arrival in Arriaga because he snored, so when he peeled another bill from the wad as I pulled up to our hotel I grabbed his wrist.

"No way, José," I said. "You were sleeping!"

"Are you saying you didn't do it?"

"Maybe I did, but so what? You couldn't hear it."

"Doesn't matter," he said calmly. "It's not about what I hear, it's about what you say. If I hear someone else cuss, are you going to pay me?"

I dropped his wrist and sat in silence to let my tongue recover from its rhetorical butt-kicking, until Peter followed up with a suggestion that slapped me out of my daylong funk—once I understood it: "*Dejaremos todas las cosas innecesarias aquí.*"

"Speak English, you little show-off!"

"If you're so worried about all the stuff in the car, let's empty it out and repack the trunk. We can leave all the junk we don't need in the hotel room."

As I stared at the mound of trouble in the rearview mirror, my mood rocketed from pit to peak so fast I thought I must be bipolar, but I didn't care because I was on the giddy end of the swing.

We took turns choosing items to abandon, and neither of us offered a single objection to the other's choices. Out went the lawn chairs, six water jugs, two cans of white gas, and a ten-pound Coleman stove. We dumped all but two of the dozen propane canisters that fit a smaller stove and transferred our bags to the trunk.

It didn't take long before the car was empty, and we went to sleep that night feeling a lot less anxious about the next day's crossing. Little did we know, however, that there was something worse than having bags in your backseat at a third-world border. His name was Pedro, and we had just made room for him.

♥ ♥ ♥

It took most of the day to cross Mexico's flat and buggy isthmus, and we approached Guatemala late in the afternoon. The final stretch of road before the El Carmen crossing was a narrow strip of blacktop fringed by a high wall of tropical vegetation, and a weird glow filtered through the trees. Though it was a huge relief to have an empty car, we were still plenty worried about what was ahead, and that slasher-movie light didn't help. Peter and I were as jumpy as caffeinated shih tzus.

Just as we rounded the final corner before the border and glimpsed the sweaty, smoky chaos on the Talismán Bridge, a shout exploded from the brush to my left. I scraped myself off the ceiling and checked the mirror. A man was sprinting into the road waving his arms.

I locked the brakes and skidded to a stop, expecting to see soldiers from a camouflaged checkpoint come flying out of the woods. Yet the only person visible as I backed up was a little guy in a wrinkled dress shirt and polyester slacks. Before I knew it, Pedro was in the backseat. He waved a big ID that hung from a chain around his neck, and he barked orders with impressive authority.

"Keep driving," he demanded, and in half a minute we reached the back end of the traffic jam.

"Go around on the right," he ordered, and his autocratic tone drowned out the little voice that told me it was a bad idea to abandon my place in line. He directed us down a ramp into a short, constricted parking lot a dozen feet below the main road, and within seconds we were surrounded by his shabby friends.

Pedro shouted at the men to back off. He had business to conduct.

"I need a hundred dollars to fix your paperwork," he said, and I knew I'd been had. One glance at the ragtag line of vehicles waiting to cross into Guatemala was proof enough that it couldn't cost anywhere near a hundred bucks. I wanted to tell Pedro to suck a tamale, but my options were limited. We were in a lot so tiny I couldn't turn around. Half a dozen men were sitting on our hood and trunk, and so many jostled for a view through our side windows that all I could see was a confusion of bad teeth and wispy mustaches.

We couldn't leave the car unattended with this crew. I had stuffed two thousand pesos into a hole in the carpet, and even if the rabble didn't break in and find it, they might slash our tires in retaliation for resisting Pedro's "help."

The ID also gave me pause. It was a high-quality placard with an official Mexican stamp. I knew the guy was gouging us, but I still couldn't swear he wasn't with the government. So I dickered him down to fifty dollars before reluctantly handing over our passports, car registration, and title.

Pedro trotted off while Peter and I slid out my side of the rapidly heating car. It was a steamy ninety degrees, and the fierce sun broiled us like ants under a magnifying glass. We were mashed against the door by a sweaty mob that grew by the minute. Gringos presented a rare opportunity for serious commerce at this tropical pit stop, and no one wanted to miss it.

"Eh, amigo, buy some quetzales," hollered a man to my left, referring to the Guatemalan currency. "I will give you the best price."

"You want a knife, amigo?" another voice shouted. "The road is very dangerous."

I swatted a boy's stealthy hand off my pants pocket, and another took a run at the one on my shirt. Peter slid so close that he was half behind me, but he used his free hand to keep away the junior pickpockets who had wormed their way among the men.

"I'm going to write down that jerk's ID number and talk to the federales when we get out of here," I grumbled.

Peter huffed. "He *is* a federale. The other guys listen to him."

When Pedro trotted back a miserable five minutes later, the ID was no longer hanging from his neck.

"You need to come with me," he said.

"What?!" I bellowed. "I gave you fifty bucks to take care of it."

Pedro just shrugged. I looked helplessly at the car, my son, and the crowd of men, each of whom was displaying his seven rotten teeth in a smile of smug satisfaction. They had seen this movie before, and they obviously loved the ending.

"Just wait a minute, damn it."

I opened the car door and leaned in, pulled the roll of pesos from its hiding place, and stuffed it into my front pants pocket. As I stepped back to close the door, Peter surprised me by sliding behind the wheel.

"I'll watch the car," he said. His voice was steady, but he looked pale. "What?"

He pulled the door closed and rolled the window to within an inch of the top.

"Go ahead. Hurry."

Over the lip of the road's steep shoulder, the top of the border building was visible about a hundred yards away—maybe fifteen seconds at a full sprint. I ducked my head and checked that all four doors were locked.

"Just go," Peter said. "It's getting hot."

I cussed, but he didn't seem to notice. "Okay," I said finally. "But lay on the horn if you need me."

Peter nodded, and I scrambled up the hill after Pedro. I would have bet that no one was aware that I was carrying so much money, but I would have lost. I guess the porn-star bulge of bills in my pants was a clear give-away since my murderous expression told one and all that I really *wasn't* happy to see them. When I glanced back at the car from the top, half the crowd was in pursuit.

At least they won't be bothering Peter, I thought as we raced past the line of traffic to the border building. Behind us, excited shouts of "gringo" and "dinero" competed with the chorus of impatient drivers' horns, and the posse grew.

A Guatemalan guard at the border handed me something to sign. "Forty quetzales," he said, and my jaw clenched. Pedro had charged me fifty dollars for a six-dollar permit and then had the cojones to stick me with the bill! I swung around to confront the little creep, but he had vanished. So I paid the bill in pesos, collected our papers, and turned to face a wall of very interested parties.

I figured the chance of getting robbed was slim unless I got caught in the middle of that mass of light-fingered Luises. So I strolled nonchalantly toward their right flank, apparently engrossed in the fine print of my Guatemalan car permit, and took off like a thief. Peter opened the door when I flew off the top of the hill, atop which a couple of persistent pursuers stood in glum resignation.

The boy was soaking wet and beet red from the heat, and he was even angrier than I was at getting rolled for fifty bucks. He still had dreams of scuba diving on this trip, but all the flimflams and shakedowns were draining the recreation pot. When Pedro's friends tried to extort a few bucks to move out of our way, Peter had another idea.

"Just run 'em over!" he growled.

Unfortunately, I still needed help to get out of the lot, so I paid thirty pesos to a man who shooed away the others so we could back up the ramp to the side of the road. He then exchanged words with the driver of a semi before trotting back to my window.

"He wants twenty pesos to let you in line."

"Son . . . of . . . a . . ." I wrestled yet another bill from my pocket. A few boys danced in front of the car while the payment was made, and one of them ran up to Peter's window.

"Give us five pesos and we will move," he said grimly.

"Move, or we will cut off your heads and put them in the trunk with the others," Peter snarled in Spanish while I was still composing a less complicated answer. The junior extortionists vanished into the traffic jam.

"What did you say about their heads?" I had to ask, and the answer made me shake mine with envy. "We didn't learn any bloodthirsty threats in my class."

I slid into line in front of the semi, and we sweated off two pounds apiece as we crawled forward to the crossing. I flashed my new permit to the guard and finally put the madness of Mexico behind us.

The condition of the asphalt instantly improved, and I took a last look in my rearview mirror through narrowed lids. With its tens of billions in oil wealth, drug money, tourist dollars, and remittances from millions of immigrants in the United States, how could Mexico have worse roads than an impoverished backwater like Guatemala? It had to be one of the most corrupt places on the planet. No wonder everyone was grumpy.

❦ ❦ ❦

The people we met on our first afternoon in Guatemala were almost too friendly. When I stopped along the side of the road to ask directions from a farmer, he let up the sheep he'd had pinned to the ground, hopped a fence, and trotted over to the car. He was a dark-skinned man in denim jeans, a long-sleeved shirt, and a straw cowboy hat, and he was so short that he barely had to bend to lean on my windowsill.

"Where are you from?" he asked cheerfully, revealing a complete set of straight white teeth.

When I told him, he launched into a description of a trip he had taken to Houston to buy an old car, which he had driven back to Guatemala, refurbished, and sold for a profit. He said a lot of other things during a ten-minute monologue punctuated by peels of girlish laughter, but I understood little of his speech and not one of his jokes. I was listening hard for instructions on how to get to Xela, as the locals call Quetzaltenango, but all I heard was a confusing stream of words that seemed unrelated to my question. I shook the man's hand, pulled back onto the asphalt, and immediately turned to my interpreter.

"What was that about a goat? It's up ahead someplace. Are we supposed to turn left at the goat?"

Peter shook his head. "There's a woman up ahead who has a son who lives in Xela. She can give us directions."

"And the goat?"

"I didn't hear anything about a goat."

"I did," I said stubbornly. "It seemed like a crucial point."

A few miles up, we pulled into the packed-dirt yard of a little wood-and-thatch shack, scattering a brood of chickens that had been pecking in the shade of some banana trees. A skinny, brown dog lay just to the left of the open doorway. It raised its mangy head and loosed a low growl, but that was the limit of its ambition on this hot afternoon.

A woman in a sweat-stained yellow dress was bent over a basin to the doorway's right, her broad back bucking with the effort of rasping a shirt against a washboard. She called something over her shoulder and continued rasping.

"I don't see any goats," I said after a few awkward seconds. "Maybe we ought to keep driving."

"This is it," Peter hissed with undisguised exasperation. "Go ahead and ask her how to get to Xela."

Just then the woman stood up, tossed the shirt into a bucket at her feet, and turned around, and my head rang with the memory of the farmer's laughter. On her thick shoulders sat a head so goatish that when she spoke instead of bleated I did a double take. Her face was long and bony with wide-set eyes, but it was the cleft palate that really did her in. Combined with a broad, flat nose whose protracted bridge began just below her hairline, it had the look of a snout.

She could not have been friendlier, though, and she was helpful as could be. She spent ten minutes explaining the key turns ahead in wonderfully languid Spanish before patiently correcting my mistakes when I repeated the instructions. As it turned out, there was only one place where we could really screw up, and unlike so many others, it featured highway signs. As long as we stayed on the main drag until then, we would have no problem reaching Xela, she said. We thanked her and pulled back onto the road.

"See? I can too understand Spanish," I crowed when we had gone a safe distance from the house.

"Uh-huh. Good," Peter replied, the way one would to a toddler showing off some catastrophe of crayon art. "I just hope we don't have to ask anyone else for help." He peered through the window at the western sky. "We don't have much time until dark."

As a rule, we were never outside at night in Latin American cities, especially ones with which we were unfamiliar, but these first Guatemalans had been so friendly that I wasn't overly concerned. I was also still celebrating my triumph of picking one word from the ten thousand uttered by the farmer, so I didn't want to hear any negativity.

"I have a feeling we aren't going to have any trouble down here," I said, and to this day I wince when I remember that ignorant proclamation. "We'll get there when we get there. Don't sweat it."

We passed a bus with a windshield even more tricked out than the Dart's, and then another one. The outside of the hand-me-down American Bluebirds were garishly painted with murals that showcased the stylized signature of the madman behind the wheel. We followed one until the driver lost patience and pulled out to pass whatever was keeping him from flooring it, and when he pulled back in, cars were scattered along the grassy shoulder. It was alarmingly clear that a Guatemalan driver's decision to pass depended not on whether vehicles were coming but on how large they were. A bus wouldn't pull into the path of another bus, but a string of cars was fair game.

As we came up behind a second bus, the back door flew open. A skinny teen stepped out, scaled a metal ladder, scuttled along the heaving roof, and swung back in through the front door. We watched other teens perform the same death-defying maneuver on other buses, but we didn't learn the reason until few days later when we took our first ride. The boys were fare collectors, and they found it preferable to risk their lives up top rather than fight their way to the front through a wall of Mayans.

There were about six million Mayans in Guatemala in 2002, and it seemed that five point nine million were always packed into whatever bus we were on. When they weren't riding buses, they liked to see how many they could cram into the bed of a compact pickup. We got stuck behind such a load soon after turning north onto the last stretch to Xela. There had to be two dozen people in the back of that little truck, and they swayed as one as we climbed from the sweltering, palm-spangled lowlands into chilly mountains draped in pines.

The winding road wasn't built for speed, and the truck moved even slower when a cold rain began beating down. Someone produced a plastic tarp, which practiced hands unfolded across the heads of the riders. The men's drab cowboy hats and women's bright woolen shawls disappeared in a flash of hunter green, and in seconds we were looking at what could have been a covered load of hay. A very short load.

"Those guys are stumpier than Mexicans," Peter said as we watched the green mass heave with the bumps and twists of the road. "You are going to be a bigger freak here than you were back there."

I couldn't argue. But being a head taller than the average Guatemalan and blond to boot, Peter wasn't going to be flying under any radar, either.

"Why don't you pass?" he asked, followed so quickly by "Oh" as a twenty-ton logging truck barreled out of the mist that it sounded like a single sentence. So we just watched the human hay bales for a couple of hours until the pickup pulled off into a village just short of Xela.

We rolled into Guatemala's second-largest city at 9:00 p.m., which despite my earlier assessment felt like a very bad time to be wandering the dark and empty streets. We had no choice, however, since we had no local currency and the manager of our flophouse for the night insisted on being paid in advance.

"The cash machine is a few blocks that way," he said. He pointed down the block toward the central square, and as we were turning to go, I paused. Instead of lowering his hand, the man had moved it to a small crucifix hanging from his neck. *Just like a scene in a Dracula movie*, I thought as we stepped off a curb onto . . . cobblestones! Now that was creepy. All we were missing were gas lamps and a wolf howl.

The ATM booth was a capsule of light in the darkness, a beacon to bad guys for blocks around. But it could have been worse. It could have been the kind of sultry summer night in which a thug could lie in ambush in comfort. Instead, it was fifty degrees and pouring rain. Surely, even the hoodlums were home on a night like this.

I learned later from perusing the local papers that Central American criminals are some of the most industrious in the world. They rise early for home invasions or to have their pick of victims at bus stops. They work late committing armed robberies from the backs of motorcycles. They are also some of the most ruthless SOBs on Earth, sometimes gunning down women for their cell phones. And, we would soon discover, they work in any kind of weather.

Peter stood watch near the locked glass door while I walked up the stairs to the machine. If he saw anyone skulking outside I was going to withdraw only a few bucks more than the ten dollars we needed for the hotel.

"Coast is clear," Peter yelled, so I took out three hundred dollars in quetzales, stuffed the bulk in my skivvies, and kept a few bills in my pocket to hand over in case of robbery. Peter and I had discussed this strategy many times since our first days in Mexico, and we never left the house without protection money. If ever we were accosted, we planned to whip a fistful of small bills from our pockets and politely hand them over, perhaps with a heartfelt "Muchas gracias, señor."

So when the guy rushed out of the darkness screaming, "Give me the money!" as we left the booth, it wasn't as if we didn't have a plan. I just ditched it in a panic and switched to Plan B:

"*Run!*"

I could have saved my breath. Peter was already five feet up the sidewalk, his skinny legs churning like an Olympic sprinter's. I gratefully thought later about all the speed work he had put in on the track in Mexico. Now, however, I was only thinking about getting him to the hotel without any new orifices.

The initial shock wore off after the first fifty yards, leaving another 150 of relatively clearheaded flight, and I slid in close behind Peter. Our escape had caught the robber by surprise, and we had a fifteen-yard lead by the time he got his shorter legs up to speed. He was hampered not only by height but also by fashion choice, and I could hear the clack of his leather boots receding on the cobblestones behind us. With a hundred yards to go I saw the manager's head sticking out of the hotel doorway. At fifty yards he started screaming gibberish and waving wildly to urge us on. When we crossed the threshold, he slammed an immense wooden door and slid home an iron bolt big enough to stop a conquistador's battering ram.

"The streets aren't safe at night," the manager admonished, and for the second time in five seconds the hotel was nearly the scene of a homicide. As I paid him his ten dollars, I fantasized about tossing him back outside to dispense his wisdom to the other guy, and as I drove behind him later to a secure garage, I had to stifle an urge to see how far the Dart could knock his scooter.

When I got back to our room, Peter was asleep in the middle of the single bed, which took up most of the space in the smallest hotel room I had ever seen. I lay on one edge of the mattress, braced my feet against a wall, and pushed him toward the other one, and in spite of this awkward arrangement, I slept a good forty-five minutes that night. The rest of the time I thought about our narrow escape, and by morning I had calmed down.

It wasn't the manager's fault that the streets weren't safe at night, and I couldn't blame him for insisting that he got paid in advance. We were in Central America now, and the risk meter had just ticked up a notch. From now on, we were just going to have to be a lot more careful.

NINE

We stood in the shadow of the hotel doorway and peered at our new world with the enthusiasm of field mice at a raptor reunion. We'd always had a vague sense that trouble was out there somewhere, but having it swoop out of a doorway and chase us up the street made it harder to ignore.

The dude in the blue jacket hustling up the far sidewalk looked like bad news, and how about that young guy in the windbreaker trotting the other way? We watched pedestrians for a good five minutes, pegging each one as a potential cutthroat before two fifty-five-pound schoolgirls strolled by and shamed us out of our sanctuary.

"Buenos días," they called and continued down the block as if they owned it. Their utter lack of concern with their surroundings was inspiring, as if we'd watched them do double flips off a diving platform from whose edge we'd been backing away. Once we took that first step, the rest didn't seem quite so scary.

After Oaxaca's heat, the morning chill was invigorating. Men dashed up and down the sidewalks with an energy we rarely saw in Mexico, and not one seemed the least bit interested in playing chicken. We strolled down to Xela's main square and found a warm patch of sunlight from which to watch the morning rush.

The square was a concrete platform with a few shade trees and benches, around which taxis raced like NASCAR's finest. On this Monday morning, a few beggars were staking out their spots along with shoeshine men, but most people were simply crossing quickly to get from one side to the other.

The buildings that bounded the square were newer than those in Oaxaca, but they appeared eons older. I had read that they were fine examples of nineteenth-century German architecture, and they were impressive. But they were also drab. They looked ancient enough to pre-date color.

"What do you think?" I asked.

"I like it," Peter responded immediately. "It's like they don't even see us."

I watched the people swarm past for a few seconds and agreed that he was spot on. Whether two white giants were not worth a second look in Xela or the residents were just extra polite, no one was staring.

We continued down the block past the ATM booth, which stood a few feet away from a bank doorway where the bandit had been hiding. Today two security guards stood there, wearing bulletproof vests and clutching shotguns. They looked worried.

With armed robbery so rampant in Central America, every business that could afford a guard had one, from restaurants to supermarkets to movie theaters. And every morning the newspapers carried stories of guards shot dead the day before. Their life expectancy fell on a scale somewhere between Chinese miners and Islamic suicide bombers.

Attacks were so frequent in some areas that a lot of citizens carried guns for protection, so shoot-outs between robbers and their would-be victims were not uncommon. It was heartening to read stories of a businessman blowing away a couple of villains, but there was also a downside to that rebellion. A lot of robbers had decided it was safer to shoot first and then search the bodies for valuables. Guatemalan cities were the Wild West, and the best defense was to stay out of the kinds of areas that our meager budget invariably forced us into.

We asked around town and found a man whose friend had a rental house a couple of miles to the west. The hundred-dollar price was right, so we took it sight unseen, collected our bags from the hotel, and set off for our new home. In contrast to Oaxaca, only a couple of Xela's downtown roads were busy. And though the sidewalks weren't much wider, pedestrians either slid past with natural consideration or stepped politely into the streets, which got emptier the farther west we walked.

I waited at an intersection for Peter, who had slowed as we passed a window full of pastries.

"This place isn't too bad, huh?" I remarked as I peered down a narrow concrete street. It was squeezed on both sides by long, low buildings faced with flaking gray plaster, and electrified wires crisscrossed the airspace from one flat roof to the other not far above our heads. You could hear them humming. "It's not as pretty as Oaxaca, but the people seem happier."

We crossed the intersection and strolled into a barrio on whose main drag not one car was moving for the half mile or so we could see. The quiet was wonderful, the atmosphere cleansed of the hostile cloud we'd choked on for the past month. Despite our rude introduction to the town the night before, I was beginning to feel at ease.

"If we stay inside at night, I don't think we'll have any more trouble," I declared, and as if on cue a zombie staggered out of an alley and glommed onto my arm. The thing had one bloodshot eye, soiled rags for clothes, and breath like diesel fuel. It slurred something incomprehensible, spraying me with TB spittle, wagged a tongue coated black with fungus, and winked its weepy, empty socket.

I shrugged the creature off and shoved it back into its lair.

"Ehhhh!" it called from the shadows as we trotted side by side up the empty street. "Ehhhhhhhhhhhhhhhhhhhh!"

"Nasty!" Peter hissed. "Naaaaasty!"

A block ahead we saw another one passed out on the sidewalk in a puddle of urine. Two more were asleep in the grass of a tiny park in the middle of a traffic roundabout, beyond which we were accosted by three semiconscious men who wanted money for another bottle of firewater.

Turns out we had rented a house in Margaritaville, and we were passing through during the daily transition between morning hangover and evening drunk. From dusk until late each night, local men sat on stoops and roamed in obnoxious bands as they consumed bottles of cheap local hooch distilled from sugarcane. In the mornings, the ones who hadn't made it home lay like corpses wherever they had fallen the night before. From about ten to two each day, the ones who hadn't frozen to death woke up and staggered home to recover.

The zombies had no homes. They had started out like the common drunks but had awakened on the sidewalk one morning too many. They had lost their jobs and then their families, and they spent whatever coins they could scrounge not on food—like the town's army of sober beggars—but on moonshine. They were the walking dead, destined soon to drop the adjective.

Oh well, just one more place I couldn't tell Peter's mother about.

♥ ♥ ♥

Our house was one of only three single-level concrete dwellings on a short cul-de-sac, across from a vacant lot where a local farmer sometimes grazed his cows. Behind us rose a mountain called El Baúl, from whose forested flanks each night slunk a snarling pack of feral dogs. There was a pretty park on top, miles up a steep and winding road, but when the crowds of weekend picnickers cleared out, it became a dicey place to walk around. Bandits occasionally lay in wait on the hiking trails.

Our home came fully furnished with two bedrooms and—most important—heavy bars on the doors and windows. Both beds sported four thick woolen blankets, which were essential because the place had no heat and we were nearly eight thousand feet above the sea. Peter was especially excited about the twelve-inch TV on the wobbly coffee table, and I was thrilled to find that our shower pipe produced hot water, even though it did so with the help of a scary contraption made of chipped plastic and bare wire.

But the best part was the quiet. No roosters rent the predawn silence, and no buses roared past the house as they had in Oaxaca. In fact, there were no vehicles at all on our street, much less one that whooped from 2:00 to 4:00 a.m. The only noise we could count on was the subtle drumming of rain on the tin-shingled roof and the not-so-subtle din from a dilapidated garbage truck that rolled past at dawn one morning a week.

And roll it did. Its rumble would rouse me on its first pass, which gave me twenty seconds to grab our trash and run for the door while the truck turned around at the end of the block. It came tearing back so fast I had to sprint to toss our bag into the bin. Hanging from the sides were a couple of filthy men whose ostensible function was to pick up garbage that residents left outside. But no one ever did on account of the stray dogs, so the men just rode.

It was so quiet in our barrio that noises that might have passed unnoticed amid the bedlam of Oaxaca could make you leap to your feet. Watchdogs patrolled the flat rooftops, and nothing could get your blood moving on a cold morning like having one lean over and snarl from a foot above your head. The explosives launched in honor of the local church's patron saint were not as frequent as Oaxaca's, but lacking any competing noise they packed ten times the punch. When one blew up above our roof at 2:00 a.m. one morning, I reenacted the levitation scene from *The Exorcist* before crashing down and biting my tongue. It even woke up Peter.

But the blasts were as infrequent as the trash truck. For most of our stay, we heard nothing more outside our walls than the occasional bawl of a grazing cow or the clack of boots on the cross street a hundred feet away. That's why, one afternoon when Peter's breath began tailing off like the feeble hiss of a geriatric snake, my ears pricked up.

"What did you say?"

Peter looked up from his homework, expression blank.

"Huh? Nothing."

He went back to his writing, and after a couple of seconds I went back to mine. We were sitting at an angle, separated by a short corner table on which sat our home's only lamp. He was wrapped in a sleeping bag at one end of the couch. I was in a padded chair, similarly wrapped. We could see our breath when we spoke, which is why I knew I wasn't hearing things. He had whispered something. His vapor cloud was just too big to have come through the relatively cool channels of his nose.

He coughed, but within the guttural expulsion I swear I detected a scrap of language.

"Did you say something?"

"Huh?" Peter looked up again, eyes wide with innocence. Too wide. The kid was messing with me.

We were coming up on dinnertime, which always raised the anxiety level in our house. We had a deal. If Peter finished his homework first, he made dinner. If I finished first, I made it. Since we were each fierce critics of the other's cooking, there was a strong incentive to rush, but Peter never did. Many a night he sat studying by the dim light of the lamp as I butchered another meal.

"How's it taste?" I would ask.

"Like dog barf," he would invariably reply. "But thank you for making it."

He was a polite kid, but even so, the gulag menu was getting to him. He coughed again. It sounded like "Daahhma." This time I didn't look up. He did it again, and a few seconds later I caught the tail end of a drawn-out whisper: "Noooooooooooesss."

"All right. I heard that. What the heck are you trying to say?"

He looked at me with the inscrutable gaze of a champion poker player, but as his head tipped toward his notebook I saw the unmistakable beginnings of a smile. I glanced back at my book, but by now I couldn't read a word. All I could do was wait, and it didn't take long.

"DaaaahmaNoooooooooesss," he whispered like a witch doctor at a pot of boiling monkey hearts. "DaaaahmaNoooooooooesss."

As in a certain famous pizza we couldn't afford.

Peter was growing fast and always hungry, but we rarely fixed anything that didn't turn the stomach. Breakfast was the worst. Our powdered milk had a stubborn reluctance to reconstitute no matter the vigor with which we shook our canteen, and the result was never better than a thin gray gruel flecked with grainy yellow balls. Our generic cornflakes were always flaccid with humidity, so the powder balls provided the meal's only crunch.

We brought cheese and bread to school to eat during the morning break, and though it was dull fare, it at least possessed a comforting consistency that was lacking in our dinners. Those were high adventures thrown together from whatever ingredients we could pick up for a buck or two in the market. For every edible accident we prepared, usually on those rare days when we splurged on a piece of meat, we concocted three stomach-turning calamities involving mushy boiled vegetables and half-cooked rice. So tonight, as Peter knew all too well, the odds were against us.

"It's getting dark," I said, and his head snapped up. "It's too late to go outside, and besides . . ."

"I know, I know," he said, and he shook his head bitterly as he returned his gaze to his schoolbook. He didn't need to hear me say what he already knew: pizza, at nearly eight bucks even in Xela, was too expensive. If we maintained our fiscal discipline for another few weeks, we would be back on budget. We could make it to the End of the Road, and we might just get a scuba lesson somewhere along the way. So even though Peter sighed deeply at the sight of his soggy vegetables that night, he ate the vile mush with only few groans and one muttered threat.

"When you're old, you're going into a home that serves this glop three times a day," he said as he tossed his empty bowl into the sink. "But thanks for making it."

Did I mention that he was a polite kid?

♥ ♥ ♥

Our school was the picture of charm. A couple dozen wooden desks were arranged amid a riot of broad-leafed plants in the open courtyard, where we and other students sat across from our respective teachers from eight to one. We sipped hot drinks until the sun crept above the lip of the roof and seduced us into shedding our coats and wandering into the break room to fill our cups with cool water. It was a beautiful place, and if not for the Spanish lessons I would have enjoyed every second of it.

The more I learned, the more stupid I felt, especially when I remembered my mistakes from the past. Some were more serious than others. For instance, I finally understood why a Mexican guy with whom I'd been trading good-natured insults in a bar years before had suddenly stiffened. I had tried to tell him he'd had too much to drink, but by employing the verb *ser* instead of *estar*, I'd called him a drunk.

I now knew why a butcher had snickered when I'd announced I wanted "to get" a pound of chicken. By employing the verb *coger*, more commonly used in those parts as a euphemism for sex, I had raised the specter of a wild night in the kitchen.

I also learned that telling a Latin woman she was "hot" was a sure way to get shanked because it carried connotations more associated with behavior than appearance. The confounded language was lousy with land mines! Who'd have thought that a compliment could get you killed or that ordering a meal might get you locked up for bestiality? It was paralyzing, and for a while I was afraid to open my mouth in public.

Peter had no such compunctions. He was chattering like a native by the end of the second week thanks to a supple young brain and a no-nonsense teacher who worked him like a mule. Learning idiomatic Spanish from the get-go gave him the advantage of never having to unlearn anything, so he didn't have to stop to think about what he was saying. His mistakes were minor, and his teacher made sure he only made them once. Her demonstrative *no*'s echoed through the courtyard.

My teacher was a short, stocky man with a brusque manner and even less patience than I had. He was a short-timer, having just a few months left before completing his master's in government administration, so he didn't feel compelled to hide the fact that he'd had his fill of babysitting tourists.

"This job puts me to sleep," Edmundo said. "If this is going to work, we cannot bore each other. You must tell me everything, and I will tell you everything."

I enthusiastically agreed, figuring I would start with some stories from our trip. But Edmundo had other ideas.

"You are married, right?"

"Yes," I said, nodding toward Peter's table. "I have two kids: Peter and Hannah."

"I don't care about your children," he said with a dismissive wave. "Tell me about your girlfriends. How many do you have?"

I told him I had none, and he called me a liar. I insisted, and he insulted my manhood. He didn't have a politically correct bone in his body, so we got along fine. And despite his distaste for the job, he was an excellent teacher, a bulldog on grammar who constantly interrupted my stories to correct mistakes.

The school's curriculum was daunting. There was no hiding in the back of a room full of students and letting the mind wander. Classes required such an increase in effort from the ones in Oaxaca that they incited the trip's first real crisis of discipline.

"This blows! Look at all this freakin' homework! We just spent five hours doing drills, and now I have to go home and work on *this* all afternoon? I want to watch Cartoon Network!"

Peter watched my tantrum silently before shutting me down with a roll of the eye and shake of the head.

"Suck it up," he said. "I thought you wanted to learn Spanish."

There was no question that he did. We had just sat across from our respective teachers for three hundred minutes, and my brain was dribbling out my ears, but he was ready for more.

So I sucked it up and kicked myself for ever opening my mouth. The kid had already absorbed more of the language in weeks than I had in two years of college, and even if that weren't enough to make me zip my undermining lip, more motivation was waiting in my email inbox.

We stopped by the school's computer room, and I logged in to my account for the first time in days. Sprinkled among the new messages were seven from my mother with subject lines ranging from "GO HOME NOW!!!!!" to "YOU ARE JEOPARDIZING YOUR MARRIAGE!!!!"

"Spam, spam, spam, spam, spam, spam, spam," I whispered in time to the mouse clicks before looking for something from Alison.

Her support for the trip had never waned, and her vicarious thrill at my descriptions of our life on the road made me feel a little sheepish. If anyone deserved a few months off, it was my incredible wife. She was at the gym every morning at 6:00 a.m., after which she worked all day at a demanding job. Every night she cooked healthy dinners and did more than her share of the cleanup. And even more than me, she had always wanted to live abroad. That she not only didn't protest but also heartily encouraged me to take off on this adventure was no surprise because she always wanted the best for others. That's why everyone loved Alison.

She and Hannah had just returned from visiting my mom in St. Louis. Seeing as how even today the mere mention of the trip sets my mother's teeth to gnashing, I can only imagine the man-bashing that went on during that weekend.

And sure enough, Alison's email lacked the warmth of the ones sent earlier in the trip. The evaporative cooler had gone out, and she'd had to climb up onto the roof to replace the pump. The dog was acting up because it wasn't getting its usual exercise. Money was tight.

In fairness to my mother, some of this was probably Alison's reaction to my most recent emails, which featured technically oriented suggestions on fixing this or that or advice on which bills to pay. Viewed from her end they must have seemed detached, especially in contrast with the loving messages I always sent to our daughter.

But whatever the cause, the email's tone was sobering. I didn't much care how anyone else viewed my rolling midlife crisis, but having my wife in my corner was important to me. So I spent a long time on my reply. I told her all about the town and the forested mountains that surrounded it. I thanked her again for letting me go on the trip and finished with an inspired line: "If you want us to come home early, we're on our way."

It was a selfless offer. It showed I cared, and I knew she would appreciate it. I slid my hand toward *send* but yanked it back as if I'd touched a hot stove.

My God, I thought. *What if she says yes?*

I wanted her support, but I wasn't ready to go home! It was clear as I studied what I'd written that I ought to do better than a travelogue, so once again I played the ace in the hole that had helped me win this vacation in the first place. "You would not recognize Peter," I wrote, and set out to cap the letter with a glowing progress report that would make all her sacrifices seem worth it.

Trouble was, most of what came to mind were changes that might just as easily have happened back home. For instance, that morning as I raced to school behind Peter, I noticed something that made me look twice.

"Hey, wait a second. C'mere," I yelled.

He stopped, turned, and stood impatiently with his hands on his hips.

"What? Tired already? Maybe if you sprung for some nourishing food once in awhile your old body wouldn't be so run down."

Sarcastic little cuss, I thought, except that suddenly he didn't look all that little.

"Come over here. Stand right in front of me," I said. I laid one hand on the top of his head and the other on the top of mine, and when I slid them away I could see that not more than four inches separated the pair. Since I stood six foot five, Peter must be at least . . .

"Impossible," I whispered.

"What?"

"You're six foot one. You were five foot nine six weeks ago. You're growing like a Chernobyl cornstalk."

"Hmm," he said.

I waited, but that was it.

"Hmmm?" I finally blurted. "*Hmmmm?*"

"Huh," he answered.

Aware that I was dangerously close to losing my lunch money, I took a deep breath before going on.

"Even if you aren't excited about leaving the realm of the little people, you might at least show some concern about that freakish rate of growth. Maybe we ought to see a doctor to make sure your thyroid isn't wigging out."

"Naw, I'm fine," he said, and he turned without another word to resume his race up the sidewalk.

"Okay, goiter-boy, suit yourself," I muttered (though I may have left that last part out of his mother's email).

He was also visibly stockier, thanks to workouts that had taken a wicked turn in Xela. We had been disappointed to learn that there was no track in our part of town, and since the only people who could run through Guatemalan streets without looking weird were robbers and the people they were chasing, we were out of luck. We also could not find anything from which to hang and do pull-ups, which bothered Peter more than I ever would have guessed. So when he spotted someone pressing dumbbells on the second floor of a strip mall in the center of town one afternoon, he was up the stairs in a flash.

The gym was an unheated, one-room throwback with some rusty dumbbells, barbells, a pull-up bar, and two stationary bikes, one of which sometimes worked. I winced as I shelled out eight dollars for two weekly passes, but I figured it would be the last gym money I'd ever have to spend. Weight-training is a whole lot harder than push-ups, and the one time Peter had tried it at home was enough to convince him it wasn't worth the effort.

An hour later, though, as I sprawled, sore and sweaty, in a corner, trying to stretch the kinks out of muscles that hadn't wrestled a barbell in weeks, Peter stalked around me like a Bulgarian strength coach.

"What? That's it? You're quitting already?" He was clearly disgusted by the very sight of me. Then he sauntered back to his twenty-pound dumbbells, scrawny arms held slightly out from his trunk as if avoiding the bulky lats he didn't actually possess.

All that was well and good, but as I worked on the email I knew I was on shaky ground. Peter would have grown taller anywhere, and I wasn't sure Alison would view his budding love of heavy metal as a payoff for all the trouble and expense. Spanish school was going well, but I had praised his progress so often earlier in the trip that it had lost its impact even on me. It seemed that we had cashed in the big-ticket positives of our adventure, and all that was left was a way for me to delay facing reality.

♥ ♥ ♥

Days passed, and Alison didn't summon us home, but some of the fuel had drained out of my tank nonetheless. Maybe my temporary insanity had run its course, because I started seeing the trip the way other people must have seen it. I began to realize that a guy in my position—cash-strapped and underemployed—blowing the family savings on a road trip was more than a little tawdry. Not that I was quite ready to call it off, but I started wanting to believe in the myth that I'd concocted at the beginning: this wasn't just some selfish lark; it had a higher purpose. I tried to believe, but I couldn't do it. Even though the experience had been good for both of us, I couldn't shake the feeling that the returns were diminishing with our bank account.

Things came to a head a few days later as we sat on our flat rooftop watching the sunset. Peter, as was usual these days, was doing most of the talking, rambling on about the latest skis he had seen on the Internet. He switched seamlessly to his second favorite topic—scuba diving—and I listened to him chatter excitedly about the best dive spots between Guatemala and Panama for a few minutes before I broke in.

"Scuba costs a lot of money," I said quietly as I stared at the flicking lights in a hillside barrio far to the south. "I'm not sure we're going to have enough to do it."

"We might, though," he said quickly.

"Yeah, we might. But we're not going to have money for all that other stuff you're talking about. I don't know if I can face starting over at the paper again, so we might have a hard time just paying the regular bills when we get back home."

Peter grunted. "Who else is going to hire you? You don't know how to do anything."

I stole a sidelong glance at the boy, and from his smirk it was clear that there was no offense intended. He was trying to make me laugh, and as with all impromptu comedy, some jokes just hit with a thud. What made this one especially bad, however, was that it was all too true. I really didn't know how to do anything.

"Good one," I said, forcing a chuckle and slapping him on the knee. I stood up and headed for the ladder. "On that note, maybe we ought to wrap up this party." We climbed down and went inside for a few hands of cards, but my heart wasn't in it, and I soon wandered off to bed.

I lay in the dark thinking about all the turns in life that had brought me to this dead end. I went way back, and it was tempting to shift some blame where I could. How about all the bad schools I'd been dragged through while we were moving around the country? I remembered a teacher in West Virginia telling my fourth-grade class that space capsules had windows so the astronauts could roll them down and get some air. And what was her response to my insistence that there was no air in outer space? "How do you know, dummy? You ever been there?"

I'd landed at a decent high school but was so far behind my peers that I avoided all the tough classes, which left me woefully unprepared for higher education. Funny thing, though: most colleges didn't think so. Turns out they had majors for people like me, and after flirting with the idea of a degree in basket weaving, I finally settled on journalism. It seemed less demanding.

I was able to slide by with a party-to-class ratio that was far more remarkable than my GPA. By the time I grew up and started thinking about the future, the die was cast. Though I wasn't in love with journalism, I had the degree, and my grades ruled out grad school. So I took a job at a little paper and spent the next two decades climbing the ladder to better jobs at bigger ones. All along the way I kept searching for a more satisfying career, but I never had the combination of experience and credentials necessary for the ones I found attractive.

I knew I was to blame for every squandered opportunity, but there in the dark it was hard not to think that things might have been different had someone shaken me by the lapels at some point when I was growing up. I wallowed in that bitter stew for a good five minutes before I finally got around to thinking about the boy in the next room. What had I done to encourage him to excel other than toss out an empty threat to send him home?

I'd been watching him do his homework for weeks since that afternoon in Mexico, but I hadn't gotten around to checking it. I'd told myself that I was showing respect by not doubting that he would hold up his end of the bargain, but I could have looked it over while he was sleeping. The truth was I'd been afraid of what I would find, and I didn't want to have to follow through and send him home.

But if he wasn't learning algebra, then he needed to go, and I did too. I had done enough damage to Peter's psyche over the years without sending him back alone in disgrace. If nothing else, he had learned to work hard on this trip, and I was going to stick with him to make sure that effort continued.

So I crept back out to the kitchen table and opened his binder. I started with his Spanish work and was pleased to see that everything was correct and neat as a pin. But since he had been getting one-on-one instruction in a subject he enjoyed, those problems were easy.

Algebra was a different matter. He had nearly failed the subject last year even with his mother standing over him every night while he did his homework. A live-in tutor couldn't help him grasp the concepts, so I had no illusions that he had picked them up on his own down here. And why hadn't I helped, one might ask? Heck, I had barely passed algebra myself. I didn't get it either.

I opened the first page of his binder feeling like a man about to read his own death sentence, but as I traced my finger across the lines, my throat got tight. The first page was perfect. I checked a few random pages farther on and had to pause to wipe my eyes. Not only was every answer correct, the graphs and computations looked as though they had been drawn by a calligrapher. The most recent assignments were the same.

I grabbed a beer from the fridge and climbed back up to the roof, and the lights on the hillside never lost their blur. I might have been a middle-aged failure whose only job prospect was an entry-level night shift, but I suddenly didn't feel like such a useless schlub. Something big was happening down here, something I had never dreamed of as I frantically packed the car in Salt Lake City. Peter's life was taking an incredible turn, and for the first time in years, I was right in the middle of it.

TEN

We began our final week in Guatemala still unsure of how we were going to get to Panama. We could drive the southern highway into El Salvador and then skirt the Pacific coast the rest of the way, or we could take a more mountainous route through Honduras. We spent hours with the maps, and the ever-helpful Edmundo was never shy about throwing in his two cents:

"The route doesn't matter. You will be killed either way. If you must go, then leave me your son and all your money. I will raise them to be good Guatemalans."

He thought we should travel by bus, an opinion seconded by Peter's teacher. When pressed, they admitted that the chances of real trouble would be low if we drove during the day, but they fed my fears that the car would be a target for every cop and border thief along the way.

"The first-class buses are very nice," Edmundo added. "The seats are large, and they all show movies. Some have pretty young women to serve you food."

Movies? Food prepared by someone other than me? Peter was sold. But I was surprisingly reluctant to abandon the Dart. I may have been quick to call it names, but deep down I respected the old workhorse. It was nearly thirty years old but still ran like the day it left the lot. It burned gas like a tank because it was built like one, as that guy in Chihuahua City found out the hard way. It was the US plates that had caused most of our trouble, which would have been the case with any vehicle.

Leaving the Dart would also require me to edit my twenty-year daydream of driving to the terminus of that last muddy jungle track and stepping down from the car like Columbus from the *Santa Maria*. Filing off a bus in a line of tired locals wasn't quite the same.

But in the end, the budget prevailed. I had to accept the fact that we didn't have enough money to drive to Panama and back to Salt Lake City.

When I mentioned the new plan in an email to Alison, however, I discovered that she had developed an unshakable opinion that Central American buses were death traps. I was dumbfounded. What did she know about the buses? She couldn't read Spanish online newspapers, so she had formed her opinion with absolutely no information.

Unless . . .

"Did you tell Mom anything about the buses down here?"

Peter was sitting at a neighboring terminal in the school's computer room, and he shot an uneasy glance my way before turning back to the screen.

"Huh? Maybe. I don't . . . hmm."

"Excuse me a minute," I said, banging my chair against his and scooting him out of the way. I perused the messages to Alison in Peter's Sent folder, and everything suddenly made sense. Interspersed among his pleas for pricey Christmas gifts were paraphrased stories from the newspapers he read each day in class. Buses had rolled into ravines at an alarming clip during our stay in Guatemala, and Peter had documented the gruesome details of every fatal accident. His most recent email, sent a couple of days earlier, was the clincher:

> We are leaving the car and going on buses. I'm not sure if that is a good idea, except for the money we save, because in the paper today it had an article about a bus falling 900 feet off a cliff and all 60 people dying. But we are going by first-class bus, so don't worry. The bus that fell did not have brakes. It was also overloaded. The first-class buses are not usually overloaded and have padded seats. Most of them also have brakes.

"Okay, that's settled." I scooted back to my computer. "We're taking the sweatbox all the way to Panama."

Peter stared glumly at the email for a few seconds before he spoke. "I sent that before I heard about the food and movies."

But the die was cast. There was nothing I could say that would change Alison's mind.

❤ ❤ ❤

Relieved of the burden of our most important decision, we concentrated on enjoying our final few days in town. On our budget that meant a lot of workouts in the gym and hikes up El Baúl, but leaving class one afternoon we saw a flier promoting an "international drink night" that evening. Students would gather at seven to share concoctions from around the world.

I had Edmundo call us a cab, and we set off to buy something to share. I considered two quart bottles of Gallo beer, but then I realized we could save close to a buck by whipping up something with the local moonshine.

"Fifty-seven cents," Peter corrected after all our ingredients were laid before us on the kitchen table. "We're going to all this trouble to save fifty-seven cents."

We mashed blackberries, honey, and oranges in a bowl, threw in some sugar and added a liter of sugarcane hooch. We divided the dusky concoction into two plastic canteens, which we labeled "Mal" and "Peor," and just before seven we stepped into the darkness to wait for the cab.

And wait.

And wait.

When the yips and snarls of a pack of strays erupted from the field at the end of our road, I suggested we go back inside and find a movie on TV. The cab obviously wasn't coming, but the dogs sure were, and even if they left us alone there were worse things on the streets at night.

The average Guatemalan's peaceful nature had made it easy to forget that the country had one of the highest rates of violent crime in the world. We walked for miles every day among polite pedestrians and exchanged friendly greetings with shopkeepers, but everything changed in late afternoon when El Baúl's shadow began to creep across the town. The streets in our end emptied, and on those rare occasions when we weren't already home, we raced the failing light back to the security of our iron bars. It was like living in a vampire movie.

Peter seemed to have forgotten the last time we had ventured out at night, or maybe he'd had one too many samples of the punch.

"Why don't we walk?" he asked, and I didn't have to think long for an answer to that one.

"You mean besides the rabid dogs? Let's see . . . ," I began. "There's the drunks that clog the only way out of the barrio every night. If by some miracle we get past them with our throats intact, we still have to walk up

Zombie Boulevard *in the freakin' dark*. And then what? Are you thinking of crossing the main square where the robbers hang out or circling around on that creepy street below the market? You remember the one, don't you? Where the guy got stabbed last week?"

But Peter wouldn't drop it. He harangued me with rapid-fire *please*s, to which I responded with high-volume *no*'s. Then he switched tacks and calmly described a plan that almost sounded fun. We would put on our darkest clothes and move silently through the night like ninjas—stopping, listening, and moving forward only after assessing the dangers ahead.

"C'mon, I already did my math for the weekend and washed all the dishes," he added, and that was the clincher. He had been working so hard for so long that I had to agree he deserved a night out. So five minutes later we were tiptoeing through a city I had sworn we would never again see after dark, and despite the chill, I was sweating.

As we rounded the first corner, I stopped and pulled Peter against the wall. At the end of the narrow street, just before the little roundabout park, the ends of a dozen cigarettes dipped and dodged in the night like fireflies. Silhouettes lurched from one shadow to another across the mouth of the street, backlit by a weak beam from the park's sixty-watt lamp.

What the hell were we doing out here?

I let Peter lead so I wouldn't lose sight of him. I also gave him both canteens. Swung by the plastic loops that connected the caps to the containers, they would make passable billy clubs if things came to that.

As we tiptoed ahead, we heard murmurs punctuated by bursts of laughter. We slipped along the side of the street to stay out of the light, but we couldn't see any better than the men we were trying to avoid. Most were sitting against the walls, which we discovered when Peter stepped on someone.

"Oops, sorry," he said and moved to the middle of the street, where the light hit him full on his blond American head. The drunks let out a collective gasp.

I gave him a shove and whispered, "Go!" but the men closed in long before we reached the open space of the roundabout. For a few scary seconds I lost him.

"Ehhhhhhhhhhhhh, amigo!" a drunk called from somewhere around my navel as another grabbed my arm. They stumbled into me, and I fell against the wall. I heard Peter yell, followed by the unmistakable "clonk" of a well-aimed canteen, and then our careful plan crumbled into a melee of shouts and shoves and wild swings. It was so dark I didn't know who was hitting whom, and I'm sure the drunks didn't either. I bulled my way off the wall and nearly went down as I trampled my new amigos, but I caught up to Peter and muscled through one last man-clog into the roundabout.

We trotted across the lighted park to the beginning of the walk's creepiest stretch, and if not for the angry hive we had just stirred up behind us, I would have turned back at first glance. The gloom of that desolate concrete corridor was broken only three times in a mile by the dim rays of antique street lamps. There wasn't a tree or blade of grass, but the moans that drifted from the alleys betrayed the presence of some uglier forms of life.

Just after we passed through the beam of the second lamp, Peter grabbed my arm.

"Listen," he whispered. We held our breaths as we strained to hear.

"What is it?" I finally hissed. "I don't hear anything."

"I heard footsteps."

We were still as stone, but other than the bark of a stray somewhere far behind us, it was silent.

I motioned to Peter to move, but we hadn't gone fifteen feet before I grabbed his arm.

"Shhhhh!"

I could have sworn I had heard steps too, but now there was nothing. And since we couldn't see beyond the cone of light beneath the lamp, it was impossible for someone on the other side to see us. It therefore made no sense that footsteps were starting and stopping when we did.

"I don't think anybody's there," Peter whispered.

"Me neither. Let's go."

But we didn't turn around. Even though we knew that the steps were in our heads, we were helpless to evict them on that eerie stretch of road. We began walking backward, eyes locked on the light. If someone were following, they would soon be revealed.

We stepped back in perfect unison, and that's how we fell. It wasn't the rotting corpse of my nightmares that tripped us, just a missing piece of sidewalk, but I still gave an unmanly yelp as I tumbled to the ground. One of the canteens clattered into the street, and the footsteps picked up speed in my mind.

I scrambled after the rolling bottle as Peter got to his feet, and since it was obvious now that we weren't cut out to be ninjas, we sprinted all the way to the edge of the central square.

We scanned the area for trouble, and just as a cold breeze nipped my sweaty neck, I spotted the glow of the ATM booth through the trees across the way. That was trouble enough for me, so we backtracked to a stygian side street and spent an extra twenty minutes working our way around on the heights above the square.

By the time we reached the school, I needed a drink. I grabbed a canteen and left Peter at the main table while I searched out Edmundo. He was leaning against a post in the shadows, sipping whiskey from a coffee cup and spying on women. His favorites, who happened to be sitting across from Peter, were a student home on break from a Cuban medical school and her teenage sister. I had to admit they were the cutest commies I'd ever seen, but I was still shaky from our walk and wanted to spend a few minutes talking about it before the conversation suffered its inevitable degeneration.

Edmundo shook his head. "Ooooooooooooh. You are lucky. It is a bad idea to walk through that end of town at night, even going forward." He took the canteen from my hand and refilled his cup. "I think maybe you are too dumb to find Panama."

He handed me the canteen, and I splashed a little liquid on my wrist, which I had cut in the fall. It burned like a branding iron. I took a big swig. Fire raced past my stomach to my feet, boomeranged off the floor, and walloped my skull like a blackjack. I wasn't blind for more than a second, but when the light returned, the room was blurry. Edmundo's mouth was open, and his eyes were wide as he stared at his cup. He was flapping one hand to cool his tongue.

"You could use this to poison bandits," he said finally. "Or set them on fire."

Bandits had been our main topic of conversation the past few days. Edmundo thought we were foolish to leave Guatemala, and he was hoping we would spend the rest of our trip in Xela.

"I think you will enjoy your vacation more if you are alive," he explained.

He always ended such proclamations with a laugh, but I could tell he was worried. I took another swig and coughed.

"See? You are not even smart enough to learn from your mistakes," he said, then took another long drink from his cup. "That's terrible!" He gasped and coughed harder than I had. "Refill, please."

He stared across the dim courtyard as I filled his cup.

"Uh-oh, Dad. Maybe your son will not be awake tomorrow." He nodded toward the party table.

I followed his eyes, but I didn't see Peter. Instead there sat an international man-about-town leaning back in his chair with his arms stretched across the tops of two others. One foot balanced jauntily on the top of a knee, and a half-empty canteen rested in his lap.

"Give me your camera," Edmundo said. "I will take a picture and send it to your mother-in-law. She will cut off your balls." He giggled, and as I took a step toward my tipsy son, he grabbed my arm.

"Ahh, leave him alone," he said. "He's already drunk. Besides, you told me he acts like a man when you treat him like one. How is he going to feel if you embarrass him in front of his girlfriends?"

He had me there. I stepped back, topped off Edmundo's cup, and took another drink. I couldn't believe how relaxed Peter was as he talked with the pretty sisters. He laughed at something the younger one said and leaned forward to refill her cup. He carefully closed the container and set it on the table, but this time he didn't lean back.

Edmundo was much more intrigued by the females, and as he watched them, he grew more animated. "Oh my! I think the girl likes your son a lot," he whispered, and I shifted my gaze to the teenager.

"See how she plays with her hair as she watches him? Look! Look! Look! She is touching his hand."

We watched from the shadows with wonder and envy until the booze was gone and the party started breaking up. The pretty girl came around the table to say good night, and I could see her disappointment when Peter stuck out his hand with the formality of a diplomat.

"I'm afraid the boy is as dumb as his father," Edmundo said wistfully. "Neither of you will make it home alive. You will be eaten by zombies."

"Zombies," I corrected.

He tried the word a few more times before giving up. "Who cares? You will die. I'm going to call you a cab."

Being the center of female attention was not something Peter had experienced before, and he was flying high on the ride home. Unfortunately, the feeling was short lived. He woke up the next morning so disfigured by angry red pustules that I recoiled when he stumbled into the kitchen. I first suspected he'd been poisoned as part of a Cuban plot to cripple American youth. Then I wondered whether he had gotten some zombie on him in the tussle with the drunks. I dragged him out to a pharmacist, who sold us tetracycline after determining it was only acne, albeit a remarkably bad case.

Peter glanced in the mirror when we got home, shrugged, and went back to bed, and it is a reflection of my obsession with the zits that I didn't dwell on the tawdry fact that my thirteen-year-old son needed to sleep off a hangover. The acne got worse over the next few days until strangers on the street grimaced at the sight, but he didn't seem to care. His growing self-esteem was not dependent on a pretty face, which was a blessing because he was one butt-ugly kid.

♥ ♥ ♥

We huddled around a map on the living room table a few nights later to plot the shortest route to Panama. "We can probably do it," I muttered finally, "but I don't think we'll be able to eat as well as we have here in Xela."

Peter choked on a gulp of tea. He was struggling to find his voice as I wondered aloud about the quality of Panamanian powdered milk when lights suddenly began dancing across our living-room drapes. We knelt on the couch and watched through the window as a Chevy sedan rolled up our street and stopped in front of our house.

"It's Rudy!" Peter said. A gray-haired man in a dress shirt and slacks stepped out of the car, and I jumped up to shepherd him inside. A friend of a family who lived near us in Salt Lake City, Rudy had been moved to tears when we had shown up on his doorstep soon after our arrival in Xela. What we hadn't realized when we left that day, however, was that Rudy assumed our visit would be followed by others. He had been walking through town for the past two weeks asking everyone he saw where the Americans lived, and this morning while we were at school he had found our house.

He told us all this without a hint of reproach, but I still apologized profusely and offered a lame excuse about how busy we had been. "But it is good to see you now," I continued. "Stay and have dinner with us."

Peter coughed. He was standing slightly behind Rudy, eyes wide with alarm. He clutched his stomach and pantomimed a sick man retching.

"Thank you, but I have come to take you to dinner," Rudy said, and Peter thrust a fist into the air. He dashed off to our rooms to get our coats and tossed me mine as he slipped outside, whistling contentedly. The slam of a car door cut off the whistle.

Rudy stared at the car and chuckled. He was still chuckling as he slid into his seat, and when he twisted around to back down our street, his eyes met Peter's, and he laughed harder. The mood lost some of its levity for Peter and me when the Chevy launched into a squealing backward transit of our street, but Rudy never stopped chortling. He raced around the corner on two wheels without so much as a hitch to check for pedestrians, gunned it up the road in reverse, and scattered a few early arrivals at Club Vino.

"We have some leftover vegetables . . . ," Peter began as Rudy paused in the roundabout to put the car in drive, but the rest was lost in the roar of the big American engine. It started raining, which cut our visibility but did nothing to diminish our velocity. By the time we were forced to slow down by a cluster of vendor carts on the edge of the giant Democracia market, I was reassessing my harsh critique of my father's driving.

I caught my breath as we crept along behind a line of traffic, and to make conversation I asked Rudy his opinion on driving to Panama. He launched into a five-minute commercial for Central American bus lines. The drivers were well-trained professionals who held the status of airline pilots. The vehicles cost millions of dollars, which was apparent in their smooth rides and luxurious interiors. They crashed less often than jetliners, and robberies were rare. In his opinion, they were the safest mode of transportation in the region.

"Besides," he said as he suddenly twisted around and began backing pell-mell toward a congested crosswalk, "the drivers down here are very dangerous."

He continued backward down an alley so constricted by parked cars that his mirror twice nicked the brick wall on the other side. He did this without hesitation, though I could see nothing through the rain-splattered window, and deftly slid into a parking space that left mere inches between his front and back bumpers.

Rudy laid out an airtight case for bus travel during our meal of fast-food chicken, and when we parted that night we had the ammo with which to take another run at Alison.

I didn't really need it, though. Once I opened with "Rudy says we ought to go by bus," the rest of my email became superfluous. Because Rudy was a Guatemalan friend of Alison's Salt Lake friend, his opinion reassured her in a way that nothing I said ever could.

So the decision to abandon the Dart was finally made, which immediately created a new dilemma: What could we do with it? Our Guatemalan permit was only good for one month, which Edmundo had gently pointed out when I showed him the paperwork a couple of days before.

"You should ask the school for your money back," he said as he shoved the papers across the desk. "An entire month here and you still can't read Spanish."

The best option on short notice was to drive back to Mexico, where we still had four months left on a six-month permit. But the prospect of burning time driving there to track down a secure place for the car was unattractive when we already had one in Xela, so I spent an hour on the couch considering other convoluted schemes. All of them involved either a round-trip drive to the border for a new permit or a bus ride to Guatemala City, where the government offices would be closed for the weekend by the time we arrived. I didn't want to think about showing up at Bureaucracy Central on Monday with expired papers.

"We probably ought to just leave it in Mexico," I mused.

"Hmmm?" Peter replied. He was bent over his math book in the living-room chair and didn't even look up.

"I said we ought to rent donkeys and ride the rest of the way."

"Uh-huh," he said.

Peter had been that way for a couple of days—so immersed in his homework that he hadn't even thought to insult my cooking. He continued writing while I drifted in and out of a nap, then closed the book with a slap that bounced my feet off the armrest.

"Done!" he crowed, and it was clear that he didn't just mean for the day. He had finished a half year of algebra in two months without a minute of help from anyone.

He was bouncing off the walls as we walked the next day to retrieve the car from the parking lot. School was behind him, and our month of penny-pinching had put us back on budget.

"Maybe we can go to the islands off Honduras and dive with the whale sharks!" he chirped as the Dart rumbled to life for the first time in a month. "Or we could fly to the Corn Islands off Nicaragua. What do you think?"

But I didn't answer. I was staring at the electrical gauge, whose drooping red pointer left no doubt that the Mexican steam cleaning had indeed murdered the alternator. Peter noticed my sick expression, leaned over for a look, and slumped back in his seat.

"How much is that going to cost?" he asked quietly, but I had a bigger concern: did we have enough juice to reach Mexico tomorrow before the battery died and the electrical system failed? Broken or not, the Dart had to be out of the country in three days to avoid a six-hundred-dollar fine.

As I wound through the narrow streets toward our house, Peter scribbled madly on a napkin half-unfolded across the dash. I was turning around at the end of our block when he leaned back and declared, "I think we're going to be okay."

He paused dramatically. I stared back with arched eyebrows.

"We have 3,243 dollars in the bank, right?" he began, and I just nodded. "With that thousand bucks you hid in the oil can the trunk, we have 4,243 dollars. That's about seventy-four fifty a day if we get home on Christmas Eve, so we're basically back on our original budget."

"I know that, but now we have to fix the car and—"

"So what could that cost?" he interrupted. "A hundred bucks? Two hundred? What if it's two hundred?" He leaned forward and scribbled a quick computation. "That would take us down to seventy-one dollars a day, which ought to be plenty once we park this gas hog."

He leaned back and smiled so broadly I could tell he was already gone, blissfully bobbing somewhere off Honduras in a warm sea full of giant, speckled fish.

I put the Dart in park, shut it down, and sat staring at the gas gauge, which showed half a tank. I'd figured on spending four hundred dollars for bus fares for the next forty days, eight hundred for lodging, and another eight hundred for food, after which we would need a thousand dollars for the drive back from Mexico to Salt Lake City. That left about twelve hundred dollars for miscellaneous expenses, which ought to be plenty even if we had to tow the freakin' car out of Guatemala.

I clapped Peter on the knee. He poked me in the ribs and leapt out of the car for a victory dance on the sidewalk in front of our house. I raised the trunk and started tossing bags and camping gear onto the street, and when I pulled the valuable carton from the case of Quaker State he whooped like a kid on a roller-coaster—which he was in a way, and even though he didn't realize it, his ride was due for another colossal drop.

Before we left home I'd rolled twenty fifty-dollar bills into a tight cylinder, wrapped it with a rubber band, and sealed it in a plastic sandwich bag. I'd put that inside two others, secured the whole thing with two more rubber bands, and hidden it in a quart of oil. It was a brilliant strategy designed to thwart even the most diligent robbers, and I was smirking like one of those insufferable smart kids on test day as I pulled the prize from the carton's oily bowels.

Peter chattered incessantly as I cut the rubber bands and unrolled the outer bag.

"We ought to head straight for the beach and get the scuba out of the way, because then we'll know exactly how much to budget for the rest."

I used my thumbs to pry open the seal and pulled out the second bag, which was every bit as brown and slick as the first.

"I'm thinking that if we play our cards right, we can get in two dives. We ought to get a discount since I'm only thirteen."

I unrolled the second bag and wrenched open the seal, and suddenly the chatter stopped. I tipped the opening toward the gutter, and Peter's exuberance drained out along with a good ounce of Quaker State.

He watched quietly as I opened the third bag and retrieved the bills, and when he saw that even the fifty buried snugly in the middle was as oily as a Louisiana pelican, he got up and shuffled slowly toward the house. After two months in a counterfeit-plagued region where merchants rejected dollars with even the smallest imperfection, he didn't need me to tell him we were Ahootlahed with a capital A.

Our budget was in even worse shape than our car when we pulled out the next morning to begin the most expensive half of our journey. I wasn't sure where our remaining bankroll would take us, but I was depressingly certain it was far short of the End of the Road.

ELEVEN

The gentle bounce of the first-class bus was like a mother's rocking chair, and fatigue hung heavy from many a passenger's eyelids. At our end of the coach, however, adolescent teasing and inane conversation made sleep difficult to come by.

Poke. Poke. Poke.

"Hey, they're starting the second half of *Bourne Identity*!"

"They never showed the first half. Let me sleep."

Poke. Poke. Poke.

"Hey, I think they're getting ready to serve us lunch."

"Really?" Wide, hopeful eyes.

"Nope."

Poke. Poke. Poke.

"Hey, let's play I Spy. I spy with my little eye . . . Hey, open your eyes, we're playing I Spy!"

I finally had to knock off the poking when Peter took a swing at me.

"What is *wrong* with you?" he growled.

It was a valid question, though maybe a little broad, but I had the answer for this particular instance. We'd had a rough time the day before, made all the rougher by my overreaction to it. Peter hadn't spoken to me since, and I was trying whatever I could think of to reconnect. This time I had really messed things up.

Yesterday had started peacefully enough. Misty tufts clung to El Baúl's piney flanks as the crippled Dart limped out of Xela. A cold rain began beating down just as we came up behind another pickup packed with Mayans, and we watched the soggy cargo for the next hour as we descended from the highlands. The rain had stopped by the time we reached the lowland pueblo of Samala, but the tropical sun was boiling puddles into mist so fast that we left the windshield wipers on. Crowds of farm folk were waiting at every crossroads for buses to take them to the weekend markets.

Where people weren't mashed together in unruly queues they were walking—women with baskets of produce on their heads, men clutching bundles of kindling, or maybe some chickens or a pig—and they waved with irritation as if we were the taxi they had called two hours before. Hitchhiking is so common in rural Guatemala, and rides so freely given, that a driver who doesn't have people spilling from the windows is considered rude. But even had we felt like testing the Dart's springs with a dozen extra riders that morning, we couldn't risk all the starting and stopping such rides would entail.

Every once in awhile, Peter leaned over to glance at the alternator needle in case by some miracle it had pulled out of its dive, and I could always tell from the way he slumped back into his corner that it was still pointing toward hell.

"The car's running fine," I said after a couple of hours on the road, as much to make myself feel better as Peter. "As long as we don't turn the car off, I think it'll just keep going."

But the truth was I had no idea how long a battery would power a car with no help from the alternator, and despite my brave talk, I had a feeling that we were close to finding out.

We hit the back of a honking line of smoke-belching vehicles about a quarter mile from the border, and I kept stealing melancholy glances at the needle as we crept forward. Barefoot and shirtless, half a dozen little boys danced in and out of the line, pursued by a muddy yellow cur with teats so full they nearly dragged on the asphalt. One of the boys waved a sucker above the dog's head to keep it close as they approached one car after another.

"We need money to feed our dog," the boy said when he reached Peter's window. "She just had puppies."

Peter handed him some coins, and we watched them speed ahead to the next car, hoping that his charity would impress the automotive gods and keep the Dart running. And it seemed that it had. It took another ten white-knuckle minutes, but we finally rolled up next to the border station. We cheered! We high-fived! I hopped out of the car and headed for the immigration office on feet so light it was all I could do not to pirouette. And just before I reached the door, a Guatemalan official strutted around the side of the building, leaned into the Dart, and shut it off.

A plaintive "Noooooo!" poured from the windows an instant after the engine died. Peter slumped against the backrest, closed his eyes, and started talking to himself. I stared glumly at the dozens of impatient drivers we had just transformed into parking lot attendants and envisioned the headline that would run when the news of this day trickled out: Two Americans Die in Border Riot.

I handed our papers to the official on his way inside and trudged back to stand next to the car. The man returned a minute later with the documents and told me to move along.

"The car is broken," I said in Spanish, to which he replied, "You have to move it."

"I can't move it because you killed it," I growled in English, and a young man I hadn't noticed leapt off a bench by the border shack and stepped between me and the bureaucrat.

"Calm down," the stranger whispered. "If you make him angry, you will be here for a long time."

Ricardo was a Guatemalan border hustler, and like his Mexican counterparts he made his living helping people negotiate with the bureaucracy. I wasn't thrilled to be dealing with another one, but we didn't have much choice. So I told him about the alternator, yelling above the cacophony of horns from the drivers behind us.

Ricardo chattered at the official, who disappeared into the station. After a long few minutes, he returned to help us push the Dart to the shoulder just past the building. Our new guide disappeared into the chaos of the Mexican side, and all we could do was wait like hooligans in the stocks beneath the glare of each passing driver.

After a while, Peter walked to the other side of the car and stood with his back to the traffic. He was mortified to find himself standing in judgment before the border rabble next to a broken car that, along with his ragged clothes, clearly marked him as a pauper. He had a little snob in him, and I figured he was daydreaming about rolling through the crossing in a gleaming SUV, tossing crisp hundreds out the window to smooth his transit. I stayed where I was and endured the glares, drawing a kind of bitter energy I surely could have done without.

Ten minutes later, Ricardo reappeared with a half-dozen weaving helpers. Under his direction, they spread out around the car and began pushing us down the steaming blacktop toward the border bridge. The guy on Peter's window frame began a boozy monologue that filled the car with tequila fumes, but he soon lost his breath and clammed up. He stumbled and fell at the halfway point, struggled to his knees, and crawled to the shade of a roadside palm. Another guy sprawled face-first across the Dart's hot trunk and rode a few feet until two of the others dragged him off by his belt and tossed him onto the shoulder.

Ricardo recruited a few kids to fill out the team, and we made it the quarter mile to Mexican customs. After I got our papers stamped, they pushed us backward to a pesticide station to get the car sprayed. The remaining drunks were sweating buckets in the humid tropical heat, and when Ricardo pointed to a junkyard at the top of a rise about a hundred yards away, they mutinied. He paid them a few pesos and went off in search of a new team.

The palm trees were beckoning, but I didn't want to close up the car in that blast furnace, and we couldn't risk walking even ten feet away if the windows were down. The border was as lousy with shabby characters as before, so we stood guard in the steam bath. I tried not to think about what all this was going to cost.

Ricardo returned with a sober mix of men and boys who pushed us to the junkyard. His friend gave us a jump start, and now it was time to settle the bill. The Mexican highwayman Pedro had taken fifty dollars, and his efforts had consisted mainly of inconveniencing us. Ricardo had provided a valuable service, and he had employees to pay. The financial anxiety made me a little loopy, and my foot slid toward the gas pedal as I eyed the junkyard gate. Most of the guys in the yard looked spry enough to dive out of the way, especially if I hit the horn first.

"One hundred quetzales," Ricardo said, and he stepped back as my wild eyes fixed on his. *One hundred what?* It took me a few seconds to do the math. The guy had saved our bacon and he was only asking for thirteen bucks? I handed him his money and fishtailed through the junkyard gate before anyone could have second thoughts.

The Dart sputtered as we drove away from the border bridge, though it ran better as we gained speed. About the time I had nursed it up to forty-five miles per hour and was feeling good about our chances of reaching town, the sandbags and machine gun turret of an army checkpoint came into view. Two soldiers sauntered out of the shade and waved us to the side of the road.

I was lightly pumping the gas pedal to keep some sputter in the dying engine when a Mexican Rambo marched up to my window.

"Get out," he ordered.

"But—"

"Turn off the car."

"The thing is, I really—"

"Now!"

The engine croaked the instant my foot left the pedal. I stepped quickly into the sandy lot, but Peter got out too slowly for the other soldier, who shoved him aside with the barrel of an assault rifle. Peter just yawned and rolled his eyes, which made my stomach roll—and not just because anyone reckless enough to use an automatic weapon as a cattle prod might not have the sense to check the safety first. It was more because an armed punk with a compulsion to prove he's the boss might take offense at his target's indifference. He might then feel compelled to mount a more impressive demonstration involving a car battery, jumper cables, and a gringo's private parts—perhaps after "discovering" illegal drugs in our car first. We were in Mexico, damn it!

I stormed over and shoved Peter away from the soldiers. All the fears and frustrations of the past two days burst out in one profane eruption, and for the first time in weeks his eyes began to glisten.

He walked away.

I felt awful.

"Aw, hell. Here," I called, trotting to catch up as I dug my hand in my pocket for some money. But Peter wouldn't take it. He just brushed past me, climbed back into the car, and shut the door.

The soldiers finished their search and called us a cab, which we rode in silence to a mechanic's shop in Tapachula. The mechanic grabbed a battery and a wrench, and we all rode back to the army post. With the new battery in place, the Dart fired up and we drove back to town.

While the mechanic sweated bullets in the hot sun to jury-rig the mismatched alternator, Peter and I walked up the block to a taco stand. The Guatemalans had warned us never to buy food on the street in Mexico, swearing that more than one stray dog had wound up in the frying pan, but we didn't listen. Whatever meat they were using was always perfectly spiced.

"I'll have the schnauzer, and my son here would like the Saint Bernard," I said in English, hoping to lighten the mood a little. The vendor just stared. Peter shook his head and moved to the shade of a nearby security wall.

A minute later I followed with six tacos on two plates.

"Could I interest you in a crisp hundred-peso bill?" I asked in as breezy a tone as I could muster. I hadn't felt so miserable in a long time.

Peter spat a wad of what looked like cat tendons into the gutter and picked at the remainder of his taco.

"Look," I said. "Cops and soldiers are God down here. If one says move, you need to do it fast, and it would be best if you did it before he had to ask."

Peter shoved the rest of the taco into his mouth and stared up the street.

"I'm really sorry I yelled at you."

He kept staring.

We wandered back to the auto yard, where I tried to pay the mechanic with two of our soiled fifty-dollar bills, but even though he was covered head to toe with oil, he didn't want the stuff on his money. So I paid him in pesos and drove the Dart to his father's house, where we left it in the middle of the foot-high weeds that constituted the place's front lawn. The house was a plywood rectangle with a roof of plastic tarps, not worth much more than the twenty dollars I offered the owner to guard the car for six weeks.

"Do you want to bet on whether the Dart is still there in December?" I asked Peter as the toothless old man shook a knife at us from his seat by the front door. He was cutting up a fish on a table he'd fashioned from the bottom half of a rusty barrel, and while he was probably just waving good-bye, the bloody blade undermined any goodwill he might have meant to convey.

Peter just grunted, and he ignored me completely for the rest of the afternoon. This morning, back on the bus, he had done nothing but sleep. He might have just been tired because we had gotten up at 5:00 a.m., but his silence was unnerving. We had been real pals for a month in Xela, and I couldn't bear the thought that we were back to square one. So I had started bugging him, but it was now clear even to me that making him angrier was probably counterproductive.

I sighed and picked up *Noticias de Chiapas*, the Tapachula newspaper, and skimmed through stories of shootings and knifings and fatal crashes. It was the same stuff that filled every tabloid south of the US border, so I halfheartedly flipped through the pages to the back. There, to my surprise, was a tale that made me sit up and pay attention. The top half of the page was a color photo of a woman in an outdoor cage. She was a Central American immigrant, and she had been behind bars in the heat and rain for a week with forty others since being captured by Mexican soldiers near the border. She claimed to have been raped by the soldiers, and other captives said they had been robbed. They would be held in the cage for a few more days and then deported.

The story would have made a nice sidebar to the boilerplate US newspaper stories about America's immigration policy. But in all my years of sifting through the AP foreign wire, I had never seen anything like it available to US readers.

I stuffed the paper between the seats. No point getting aggravated about something I would never be able to change. Since it looked like I was destined to spend the rest of my career at a newspaper, I'd better get my mind right and stop rocking the boat.

I turned to the window and watched the green wall whiz past, broken now and then by thatched huts and fields of banana trees. It was beautiful, and until we reached the homely Guatemalan capital and passed a city bus with bullet holes in the back door, it was hard to believe that two hundred thousand people had died in a civil war that had ended just a few years earlier. Now the country was in the early stages of a drug war made especially bloody because of all the military weapons still floating around the countryside. Government corruption and a young, impoverished populace didn't help matters. The TV news ran tape almost daily of bullet-riddled SUVs and corpses, and all indications were that the worst was yet to come.

We stopped for lunch in Guatemala City halfway through a tape of *Ocean's Eleven*. Five minutes after we left, a scratchy copy of *Shrek* came on the screen. No one complained. Following the path of least resistance through Guatemala's tortured topography, we traveled southeast from the capital, turned northeast for a stretch, then dove almost due south at Las Crucitas.

We reached the El Salvador border at the bottom of a forested river valley, and with no possessions to defend we had the luxury of enjoying the chaos. We strolled across the packed-dirt lot to the immigration trailer amid a swarm of shouting money changers. They were selling US dollars, El Salvador's official currency, so I traded my last quetzales and bought some cheesy pupusas from a woman at an open cook fire. I was thinking about our polluted stash of greenbacks as we passed another woman selling bars of homemade soap. I bought one and led Peter back to the bus.

Though I had cleaned the worst of the oil from our cash in the kitchen sink in Xela, it was still too slick and smelly to spend. Now I discretely transferred a few bills to my plastic water bottle and slid the soap through the wide mouth. After securing the lid, I handed it to Peter, who stared back quizzically.

"Shake it," I said. "When your teachers ask what you did on your vacation you can add money laundering to your list."

Nothing. Not a grunt, a groan, or even a roll of the eyes. The kid was still ticked beyond words, so I took back the canteen and let him go to sleep. I shook the soapy concoction for two hours, certain that the bills would emerge as good as new. They had to. We didn't have any others, an alarming fact that finally got Peter to break his vow of silence.

"You have the organizational skills of a Down's Syndrome dog," he declared when I confessed that aside from our oil money we had nothing with which to buy food or rent a room. "You got to Guatemala with no cash except two thousand Mexican pesos, which you're still hauling around, and even though El Salvador uses the same money we do, you don't have any of it." He shook his head, a look of pure incredulity on his face.

It was the kind of rant I might have leveled at him in the not-too-distant past, and now it was my turn to clam up. But what could I say in my defense? He was right about all of it, so I sat there shaking my bottle and praying that the bills would come out clean.

We reached San Salvador at dusk, and from the shabby, low buildings we passed as we wove through the narrow streets, I correctly guessed we weren't heading for the capital's garden spot. The Hotel San Pablo was a two-story, blue plaster hellhole with a manager whose demeanor perfectly matched her surroundings.

The sharp-faced old woman was sitting behind a card table when we walked through the door. Next to her sat a battered cardboard cigar box that she used as a cash register. When I offered her a fifty still damp from the wash, she snatched it, sniffed it, and tossed it onto the table in one quick motion. Then she pointed to the door. "The bank is a few blocks to the north," she said. "It has a cash machine."

I peered through the doorway into the gloomy street. Of all Central American slums, none scared me more than those in San Salvador. They were the breeding ground of the brutal MS-13 street gang, infamous for leaving rivals' severed heads in public parks and massacring riders on city buses.

"Is it safe to go outside at night?" Peter asked the woman.

"No," she answered without a second's hesitation.

I stuck my head out the doorway and looked both ways. The yellow glow from the low-watt streetlamps gave the empty street a sinister look. I'd have preferred the complete darkness of some of Xela's streets. I turned back to the old witch.

"If you take this money, which is real despite its smell, I will pay you ten bucks extra."

She groaned with irritation, heaved herself out of her chair, and disappeared through a door behind her. I glanced at Peter, and our nervous eyes met before I turned again to the deserted street.

"Why don't you wait for me here?" I suggested, but with a "let's get this over with" shake of his head, he stepped through the doorway. I was halfway out myself when the old woman's voice boomed behind me.

"Where are you going? Are you crazy?!"

"But you said—"

"A taxi is coming. Wait inside, for the love of God!"

So we sat on the stairs to the rooms and waited, and my mind returned to our oily thousand dollars. If we couldn't figure out a way to get that stink out, we would have to turn for home in about two weeks. I asked the old woman her opinion, but she just shrugged. I tried the cabbie, who fell silent for the entire drive across town to a safe ATM while he pondered the problem. When I got back in the cab and asked him to stop someplace where I could pick up some beer, it was as if I'd pushed a button in his head.

"Rum!" he exclaimed with a big smile.

"Pardon me?"

"Your money. Soak it in rum."

He said it with such conviction that I was convinced our troubles were over. So the next morning, when Peter pulled a bill from the booze bath in the sink, I wasn't prepared for his pessimistic critique.

"It's probably still too dark, but we might be able to pass it in a place with bad lights," he said as he held it up to the window. He jerked his head as he brought it near his nose. "Phew! It smells like zombie!"

"Gimme that!" I jumped off the bed and snatched the fifty. This had to work. I patted the bill on a bath towel, waved it above the bedside lamp for a few minutes until it was dry, and took another sniff. I handed it to Peter.

"Here, what do you smell now?"

Peter waved the bill under his nose for a second before tossing it onto the bed.

"Oil . . . rum . . . I don't know," he said. "But it's gross."

I was afraid of that. I pulled another bill from the sink and sniffed it repeatedly as I paced around the room. "We just can't ever let them dry," I declared. "They seem almost normal right out of the sink."

"Except for the color, moisture, and stench, you mean."

"Yeah, well . . ."

Still, for reasons I couldn't put into words, I was convinced that rum money was a big step up from oil money. So we put three hundred dollars in a plastic bag, added a splash of hooch, and headed out into the bright morning.

I was wrong, of course. Latin American businesses and banks were just too skittish to take US bills that weren't perfect, and ours were perfectly weird. A bank cashier sniffed one and held it up to a light before calling her manager. He repeated the steps before sliding the bill back under the bulletproof glass with a shake of his head.

Even in a bar, where a bill that smelled a little rummy should not have seemed out of place, our money was rejected. A dry fifty would have been hard enough to pass in a dump where my beer cost less than Peter's soda, but ours was inexplicably liquored up. The bartender tossed it back and made me pay the tab with a dry dollar.

As we sipped our drinks, we worked out a better plan. At the next joint I would sit at the bar and order a glass of rum. Peter would hang out near the door until the bartender served me, and at that instant stroll up to order a soda. While the guy was busy with Peter's order, I would "accidentally" spill my drink on a fifty. That would explain the soggy money, and my only hurdle would be persuading the guy to take such a large denomination.

We walked a few blocks until we found another tavern, a dark and shabby place with two battered swinging shutters for doors. Peter stopped just inside as if to admire a bikini babe on a poster-size beer ad while I walked to the middle of a long bar fashioned from planks of rough pine. At either end perched lone men nodding over half-filled glasses, and others sat alone at three of the tavern's wooden tables. No one looked up as I took a stool.

The first part of our plan went off without a hitch, and as the bartender set down my glass I waited for Peter's one line: "Give me a Coke, please," delivered with a clarity that would make his Spanish teachers proud. Instead, I heard "A Pilsener in a bottle, cowboy, well-chilled." It was the slogan on the beach babe's beer poster!

My head snapped up and left. Peter was facing straight ahead, grinning slightly. His head never moved, but his sparkling eyes rolled down and right to meet mine, and his smile broadened. I was so astonished that I forgot to spill my drink, so Peter reached down and doused the bill, the bar, and my shirt just as the bartender turned around.

The man stared at Peter a long three seconds before looking at me.

"How old is he?"

"Uhh . . . sixteen?"

"He has to be eighteen to drink this," the man said, sliding the beer in front of me and picking up the soggy fifty.

"Don't you have anything smaller?" he asked with irritation.

"Err . . . uh . . ." I patted my pockets. "No, I'm sorry. That's all I have."

The bartender exhaled heavily as he held the bill up to the light above the cash register to check the watermark, then popped it into the box and returned with $48.75 in change. I dropped a nice tip on the bar, and we headed out to find another tavern.

The scheme worked even better when Peter stuck to the script, though so many bartenders refused to break such a large bill that we did a lot of walking for our money. We wandered all the way from our seedy end of town into the nice business district where we had visited the ATM the night before, which created another complication. Our ratty clothes—wet and stained and reeking of spilled liquor—attracted such scrutiny in the only upscale bar we entered that we didn't dare attempt our scam. We left without ordering and headed back toward the slum from which we had come.

It was a long day, but when it was over our pockets were bulging with nearly two hundred dollars in clean small bills. We still had a lot more oil money to dispose of, but knowing we could do it was a load off our minds—especially Peter's. Though he was still mad at me, the sight of all that money put him in a festive mood.

"No more hotels without screens!" he crowed, tossing a fistful of cash into the air and watching it flutter back down to the bed.

Panama's currency, like El Salvador's, was the US dollar, so we would have plenty of opportunities there to run our bar drill. I was feeling more confident now that we could get to the End of the Road and back as long as we didn't go on a spending spree.

"We can eat in restaurants that use forks!" he crooned.

We were still on a tight budget, after all.

"First-class all the way from here on out. Right, Dad?"

We weren't exactly the Rockefellers.

"Right, Dad?"

We were a only step above indigent, if you got right down to it.

"Dad?"

TWELVE

To call me frugal was like saying the Boston Strangler didn't relate well to women. My six-hundred-dollar Dodge Dart was an upgrade from the bare-bones Geo Metro I had driven before, and I still had most of my college clothes. One of my greatest joys was contemplating some unnecessary purchase before walking away, and the closer I came to buying before bailing out, the happier I was. Part of it was probably my anemic newspaper paycheck, but a lot was that I never got much satisfaction from owning stuff. I came from thrifty parents and married a thrifty woman whose father was even cheaper than I was, and I loved having money in the bank.

Peter and I were the financial odd couple. While for him our rum-money windfall inspired dreams of the high life, for me it represented peace of mind—a peace that would last only as long as I had the cash in my pocket. So after learning of a budget bus line to Nicaragua, I got us up at six to lug our backpacks halfway across town.

"First-class tourists take taxis," Peter grumbled as we stepped off the curb into the trash-strewn street to avoid a sleeping drunk.

"If we save a few bucks, we'll do stuff that's a lot more fun than riding in taxis."

"Like diving?

"I was going to say eating."

We turned a corner and surprised some men just waking up on beds of cardboard, and their rapacious stares sent a shot of adrenaline through my veins. Everyone tensed, but when the men glanced around and saw the streets peppered with witnesses, they settled back down on their mats.

"Why, once again, did we bring so much stuff?" I whispered as we walked away, suddenly feeling the vulnerability I thought we had left in Mexico with the Dart. All we had really accomplished was to trade our rolling consignment store for two smaller ones that we had to strap to our backs.

The days get hot fast in the tropics, and by 6:30 we were melting under our loads. I kept looking for a place to buy water, but other than a couple of bars that we didn't dare show our faces in again, we were out of luck. By the time we reached the bus office, Peter was madder than a wet hornet—and wetter. His T-shirt was soaked from top to bottom. He dropped his pack on the sidewalk with an oath.

"This bus better have air-conditioning," he warned as he watched me arrange my pack atop his just to the left of the entrance. When I didn't answer, he poked my shoulder.

"Hey, Mr. Cheapskate. How much would you pay right now for a cold bottle of water?"

"Aw, heck, at least five bucks," I answered without thinking, and he sprang like a mongoose at a cobra.

"So you'd pay five bucks to replace the water we sweated out for an hour to save, what, four bucks?"

Cab fare was closer to three bucks, but with the way his eyes blazed and the tendons reared up on his forearms above his balled fists, I thought it best to keep that tidbit to myself. Besides, once he found out that the bus had no AC, things were bound to get ugly.

The lone ticket seller sat behind a window about twenty feet from the open door, and I joined an unruly queue of buyers jostling to improve their position. We would have to show passports to buy the tickets, and I wasn't sure a minor could make the purchase, so I reluctantly left Peter sitting atop the packs. I kept glancing back at the open door, which was never more than a few feet away, and though I couldn't see him, I was confident that I could hear him if he needed me.

And I was right. His voice echoed through the office when I was just a few spots from the front, though it was nothing like the sound of my fears. There was no terrified "Help, Dad!"—just a hundred-decibel *Bastard!*" followed by grunts and unintelligible oaths. I turned the office into a bowling alley as I plowed for the door, and an angry chorus from the unappreciative "pins" followed me outside.

Peter was dusting himself off, none the worse for wear except for a torn shirt and an angry red mark on the side of his forehead. My eyes swung so wildly in search of trouble that a man approaching on a sidewalk spun on his heel and trotted the other way. I looked behind me and spotted the attacker, fifty yards into a full-tilt sprint back to Crookville.

"What happened? Are you okay?" I asked, suddenly weak in the knees.

"He tried to take my pack," Peter replied calmly as he inspected the hole his shirt.

I waited for some details, but that was it. He was still mad at me, I figured, and the fight hadn't improved his mood.

An older woman who had witnessed the attack approached and began clucking over Peter like a mother hen. She straightened his shirt and reached up to brush back his hair for a better look at his scrape, all the while offering a gentle monologue of encouragement. When she was satisfied that he was okay, she turned to me.

"The boy is strong," she said, and I felt a fierce flare of pride, which she doused just as quickly by adding, "But you are lucky that the man didn't stab him."

Way to spoil the moment, lady.

Peter never said another word about the incident, and I didn't press it. I was mortified to have put him in such a tough spot, but I was also proud that he had handled it and gratified to see that he wasn't a braggart. I'd never said much about my own scrapes over the years, even after two drifters wandered onto my first job's loading dock to threaten the women who bundled the newspapers. When the police arrived to collect the men, one of whom had abruptly lost his ability to stand, I walked back to the office without a word and finished my city council article.

But there's the difference between me and Peter. I never forgot my run-in with miscreants, and here I am bragging about it. When I checked the date in Peter's journal years later, however, I found a rambling paragraph about the skis he wanted but nothing about fighting off a mugger on a third-world street corner. It was just never that important to him.

♥ ♥ ♥

Even though it was broad daylight, I paid for a cab to the Tica Bus office and bought two first-class tickets to Managua. The bus was luxurious, with wide seats and doilies on the headrests, and the driver played entire movies at a time.

Peter took an admiring inventory of all the amenities, yawned, and tipped his seat back for a nap. With my wallet still stinging from the twenty-seven dollars I had just dropped on our fares, I couldn't believe what I was seeing.

"Hey!" I protested. "What do you care what kind of bus you're on if you're going to sleep? It's just going to look like the inside of your freakin' eyelids!"

He just smiled and burrowed deeper into his seat. The idea of first class was enough for him, and within two minutes he was out.

I spent the next five seconds planning his dinner menu for the next two months—rice and beans on even days, beans and rice on the others—then turned to watch the scenery. We sped through the lush farmland of El Salvador and across the narrow thumb of Honduras that juts down to the Pacific, but in Nicaragua the bus suddenly braked hard and dropped with a heavy bounce off the lip of the last asphalt we would see for hours. We crept along a bumpy dirt-and-gravel strip at ten miles per hour past an impressive string of denuded volcanoes on the vast Pacific plain. It would have been a horrible place to get a flat, and I wondered how the Dart with its cheap city retreads would have handled that rutted track.

We passed a shirtless man in nylon gym shorts in a wooden cart piled high with kindling he had scrounged from a nature reserve we had passed an hour back. Pulling it was the skinniest horse I'd ever seen, and the man—who was just as skinny—whipped the beast with a pitiless gusto. The bus wasn't going much faster than the cart, and during the half minute it took us to pass, the man used his whip half a dozen times.

The lout's cruel eyes met mine as we rolled past, and I forced myself to wipe the disgust off my face. I had no doubt who would pay the price if I made him mad.

Why so skinny and why so cruel? Aside from the fact that he lived in Nicaragua, where even today barely 1 percent of the country's six million people are immigrants who live there by choice, he was heading for Chinandega. The town had a history of bad luck even by Nicaraguan standards, starting with a bombardment in the 1928 revolution that leveled most of its colonial buildings and left it off the lucrative tourist trail. Then, in 1998, Hurricane Mitch hovered above the town for more than a week, dumping feet of water and washing away homes, bridges, and the crops that the people relied on to scrape out a living.

On top of that heap of misery squatted the country's bitter political grudges, which made those in America seem petty. On one side were the Sandinistas, who had overthrown the government in 1979, seized private property for redistribution, and put the fear of godless communism into US leaders. On the other side were the crony-capitalists, once represented by the so-called Contras in a bloody proxy war between the United States and the Soviets that had ended about a decade before.

I wondered if the horse-beater was a former Contra, a Sandinista, or just a guy hacked off from years of dodging bombs and ducking bullets. I tended to think that a thug who abused his power over a helpless animal would go with the side that seized other people's possessions. Coercion is the tool of choice for those who demand something for nothing, because . . .

"Hey, Dad."

"Hmmm?"

"Are you going to buy me new ski goggles when we get back?"

"No."

He snorted with disgust. "You just remember this in a few years when I *take* your money and put you in a home."

. . . But what did I know anyway? The capitalists had had their chance to run things for twelve years, and the country wasn't much better off.

It turned out that not everyone in Chinandega was grumpy. I watched a young man nearly burst with joy at the sight of his middle-aged doppelganger stepping off the bus. Father and son embraced and took turns talking while the other struggled to contain his excitement. They walked off laughing hard, one's arm over the other's shoulder, and I'd wager that better friends did not exist.

When I turned from the window, Peter was back asleep, and for a long while I watched him.

How many times had I seen that pose years before as we drove into the Utah desert? Turning on a motor seemed to turn his off, but when the car shut down he was raring to go. He was dead to the world one time as I pulled up to our favorite trailhead, but as I stopped the car, his little head popped up and he yanked the pacifier from his mouth.

"Yup, this is the place!" he announced, adjusting his diaper with one hand as he replaced his pacifier with the other, and he was out the door before I could open mine.

He looked as tranquil as a well-fed baby curled up on the bus seat, so unlike the first time I'd seen him sleeping. There was something wrong with his tiny lungs when he arrived three weeks early, and he spent his first week in an incubator.

I'd have given anything to carry him home to his mother, but I couldn't even pick him up. I'd stare at his skinny pink frame through the plastic box for an hour after my night shift ended, and if I couldn't sleep I'd drive back over for another look. I murmured till dawn one night about all the fun we would have together, what pals we would always be.

I thought again of the father and son in Chinandega, sighed, and turned back to the window.

♥ ♥ ♥

A lot of the air had gone out of our balloon on the side of that Mexican highway, and the mood did not improve as we bounced around Nicaragua for a few forgettable days. Peter's happy chatter from our time in Xela was gone, and when he spoke to me at all he sounded like I used to when I was browbeating him. Aggravating matters, as always, was our lack of money.

We moved south into Costa Rica, where we hunkered down in a San Jose hotel for a day and a half as we tried to figure out which of the nation's many charms to take advantage of first. Of course, we couldn't afford any of the big-ticket attractions like zip lines or canopy tours. We couldn't stay long in the capital, either, where our hotel cost twenty-five dollars and even the cheapest meals were a few bucks apiece. And don't even get me started about the prices in the Pacific beach towns!

"Then let's just move on to Panama if everything's so expensive," Peter huffed after I'd shot down his suggestion for a ride on a white-water raft. "If we can't stay here and we can't afford to *do* anything, let's just go."

He dropped onto his bed, snatched up the remote, and brandished it like a pistol at the TV. He cycled through one Spanish channel after another for the next fifteen minutes, not realizing when he had reached the beginning of the circle or simply not caring.

Trying my best to block out the staccato backdrop of the fast-changing channels, I picked up the map and stared. There had to be *something* we could do in Costa Rica that wouldn't break the bank. My eye scanned the paper until it settled on a familiar thumb of land jutting into the Pacific near the Panama border. I'd hiked across the Osa Peninsula with Alison a decade before, and while it was easily the wettest, muddiest, and buggiest place I'd ever seen, it was also one of the most beautiful. Best of all, the park accommodations were dirt cheap.

I stole a glance at Peter, who, despite his frustration, was relishing the first air-conditioned room he'd seen in more than two months. He wasn't going to like the idea of trading this for some rustic hut in a sweaty bug factory. I figured it was best to go easy on the details.

"Okay then," I said after I'd had a chance to collect my thoughts. "Let's head on down toward Panama tomorrow."

He snapped off the TV and dropped the remote on the bed.

"Toward?" His eyes narrowed. "What do you mean toward?"

"I mean the Pacific coast. Beaches, palm trees . . ."

"Air-conditioning?"

I picked up the map again as if assessing the possibilities. "Hmmm, well, they might not be set up for that in Corcovado Park, but we can check around."

Peter glared silently before shaking his head, flopping back against his pillows, and snatching up the remote.

I pretended to study the map as the pell-mell tour of Costa Rican television resumed.

THIRTEEN

The Mountain of Death was socked in with clouds when our bus completed its long climb from Costa Rica's central plateau. A tall pair of oncoming headlights gave me a few sick moments, but long before the rest of the semi materialized from the fog the driver swung around a pothole and back into his lane. Before long he was back on the wrong side, but by then so were we. The pass was so badly washed out and cratered that traffic in both directions wove drunkenly from side to side in search of the least bumpy path.

Our bus's fiberglass benches provided no cushion for the jolts, but that wasn't their worst attribute. On the eleven-thousand-foot descent to the coast, each hairpin turn sent riders sliding like hockey pucks from one side of the slippery bench to the other. This complicated Peter's plans for a nap, though he made a series of stubborn efforts that finally ended with him standing on his head in the aisle.

When the eight-hour ride came to a merciful end in a muddy lot in Puerto Jimenez, he seemed to take the first torrid slap of humid air as a personal insult. The town was "Appalachia by the Sea," our two-dollar dinner of fried fish and plantains was "hobo food," and our twelve-dollar room—a fifteen-by-fifteen hotbox with one double bed and a broken fan—was "child abuse."

I had ignored his snarky critique of our rice-and-eggs breakfast, the grumbling about our hour-long slog to the station, and the moaning about the bargain bus line, but I'd finally had enough. We had been heading for a clash for days, and though I remembered my promise to keep my cool, it was time to get a few things straight.

Peter was on the bed with his back to the wall and his feet dangling off the side. I took a chair from beneath a wobbly wooden desk near the door, slid it against the far wall, and sat with my feet propped on the bed's thin sheet.

"It's good you found a place to sleep," he said. "There's barely enough room here for me."

"Would you rather be home?" I asked quietly.

"I'd rather be in a hotel with two beds and air-conditioning," he fired back, and I could tell he believed he had crushed my question like Federer with a lob at the net. I was ready for that one, though, and I tapped another one his way.

"We can't afford two beds and air-conditioning," I said. "The choice is between this hotel and home, with another adventure tomorrow or just another day at school."

"Some adventure," he muttered, moving his eyes from the cracked plaster walls to the bare lightbulb dangling amid a swarm of flying insects.

Let's get your ungrateful butt home then, I thought, but I bit my tongue just in time. I took a deep breath and let his last words hang in the silence like a mud-splattered sheet on a backyard clothesline. As tempted as I was to fling my own mud, I knew it wouldn't solve anything. I didn't want him to go home, yet I didn't want to listen to six more weeks of complaining. And that tone! Though I could see the cosmic justice in our role reversal, I couldn't take it. Even Ebenezer Scrooge had only had to face his sins for one night. We had to settle this.

"Your Mom and I have never made a ton of money," I began. "It's been hard to save much, even the way we live. We almost never go out to eat. We don't have cable TV or cell phones. We drive old cars."

Peter watched me impassively for a few seconds before raising his eyes to the wall above my head.

"So saving up that nine thousand dollars we started with wasn't easy," I continued, and despite my best efforts, a little emotion began to creep into my voice. "It involved a lot of sacrifices, and Mom was incredibly generous to let us take the whole wad. She worked damned hard for that money, and she could have said, 'Hell no; I want to use some of that on me.' But she didn't. She decided to let us have an experience we'll remember for the rest of our lives. And instead of being *grateful*, and instead of understanding how *lucky* you are to be seeing new things every day instead of the same four walls of your classroom, all you can do is look for reasons to *bitch*!"

I stood up and took another breath. I had to get out of there before I started punctuating my lecture with unhelpful phrases like "you little pain in the ass." I slid the chair back beneath the desk and stepped to the door.

Peter watched me move with growing alarm. In the past ten weeks we had been together night and day, and the few times I'd left him, we'd made detailed plans for the unlikely event that I didn't return within the hour.

"Where are you going?" he asked, and as he slid toward the edge of the bed, I raised my hand like a traffic cop.

"You stay here. While I'm gone, I want you to think about whether you can enjoy the rest of this trip or whether you'd rather go home. There are flights out of San Jose every day."

I turned, shut the door, and walked half a mile through the dark streets to a little store on the edge of town. I bought a beer and sat on the concrete curb to drink it, and when it was gone I bought another one.

I wasn't sure what Peter would choose, but the odds were with the quick flight home over six more weeks of buses, bad food, and rough hotels. I figured his ticket would cost about eight hundred dollars, which would knock a lethal hole in my budget. I would recoup a little of that on meals and by buying one bus ticket instead of two, but we were already staying in the cheapest hotels I could find. And the Dart's gas bill would be the same whether he was along or not.

Even if I could swing it, though, I wasn't sure I wanted to try. I felt old and tired as I thought of traveling alone for all those miles to the End of the Road. If Peter flew home, I'd probably just give up and catch the first bus north.

I returned the empty bottles to the counter and walked slowly back along the dark street toward the hotel. Enough light seeped out from the drawn shades of the barred windows along the block that I could tell no one else was out. Everyone was inside with their families, probably sharing pleasant stories about their day over dinner and enjoying each other's company. I cocked my head in hopes of catching a waft of muffled music or laughter as I passed, but the only sound was the crush of sand beneath my sandals.

I sighed as I turned the corner and stared up another dark street, but this one wasn't empty. Another shadow was shuffling its way toward me, probably some friendless drunk on his way to the market for a quart of Imperial cerveza. He was a big one, a lot taller than most Costa Ricans, and I tensed as we drew near.

I never gave much thought to the malnourished squirts I encountered on Central American streets, but a guy that size could be trouble. I slid to the far right side of the street and was dismayed to watch the shadow mirror my move. He was coming right for me, and I figured anyone with the cojones to take on a six-foot-five stranger in the dark had to be one tough SOB. *Or armed*, I realized as I frantically scanned the ground for a rock or a stick or anything I could use as a weapon.

Nada. I leaned down and came up with two fists full of sand, thinking I might have a chance to chuck some in the guy's eyes when he leaned in with his shank.

We were twenty feet away when the shadow passed a shaded window and a dim square of light fell across his blond hair. I dropped the sand and wiped my hands, ears burning with embarrassment but awash in relief.

"What are you doing out here?" I croaked. I could have used another beer.

Peter ignored the question, and his words came tumbling out in one choppy sentence. "I'm sorry about everything I said—I love this trip—I'm grateful that you and Mom let me come—I shouldn't have been complaining—I won't do it again."

He stopped to take a breath, and I walked up to lay my arm across his shoulder. I eased him around and started back toward the hotel, and neither of us spoke for a few awkward seconds.

"Well, that's a relief," I finally managed. "These last ten weeks wouldn't have been any fun alone. I was thinking that if you went home I'd probably just turn around too."

He slid his arm across my shoulder, and we hobbled up the street like conjoined twins.

"You scared the crap out of me," I said after a few steps. "I thought you were some kind of Costa Rican mutant."

"Really?" He sounded pleased.

"Absolutely. I didn't realize how freakin' big you've gotten until I saw you filling up half the street."

"Huh," he said thoughtfully.

"Huh what?"

"You didn't look all that big to me."

♥ ♥ ♥

We got up before dawn and transferred all we would need for the next few days into one backpack. We left the other with the hotel owner, and even though it committed us to another night in the miserable room, Peter didn't bat an eye. He volunteered to carry the pack to a restaurant, where he choked down his rice and eggs without a word.

We caught a ride in a pickup bed to Carate, a tiny village at the end of a dirt road about a mile from the edge of Corcovado National Park.

We shared the truck with two European couples and a middle-aged local man who boasted of fathering seven children by seven different women, none of whom he had married. Better yet, the stud had recently knocked up his sixteen-year-old girlfriend.

I thought of my teacher in Oaxaca, who had laughed when I repeated the widespread US notion that Latin Americans were natural family men.

"If you mean that they father a lot of children, that is true," Janet had said, adding that many fathers went north after awhile to start new families in the United States, leaving teenage mothers to fend for themselves. The abandoned girls often became the paramours of older married men in return for support.

I mentioned that I had run across a sixty-year-old American retiree with an eighteen-year-old Mexican wife, and I leaned back in anticipation of an explosion of feminine outrage. But it never came.

"The girl is lucky," she said. "The man has money and probably does not beat her. He probably is not an alcoholic either."

There was no doubt about the man in the truck. Though it was barely daybreak, he reeked of booze, and his words dripped out in slurred clumps. The truck bounced along until it reached a pretty beach where the ragged Romeo climbed out and wandered into the forest to check on his still. The Europeans immediately stripped down for a swim in the eighty-five-degree water, but Peter and the pack, and we set off for the Sirena research station. There were a couple of points on the fourteen-mile hike where a high tide would block the way, so we wanted to make sure to get past them before the ocean cut us off.

The jungle looked like a towering green wave frozen an instant before

crashing into the sea. Haystack rocks festooned with palms and hanging plants dotted the impossibly blue ocean, and we didn't see a human footprint on the whole hike. We saw plenty of other prints, though, including cat tracks the size of my hand. Monkeys chattered from the trees, and scarlet macaws flew low in squawking crimson flocks. It was the most beautiful and exotic tropical setting imaginable, and the miles flew by until we reached the banks of the Rio Claro, which was full to the brim.

We sat down to assess the obstacle. I had read that sharks swam up the Claro to feed at high tide, and the river was also home to crocodiles. So after some consultation, we decided that the prudent course was to sit back and wait for the Europeans. With luck, one would attempt the swim and help us better assess the predator situation.

But the hours passed and no one came. Finally, late in the afternoon, the river began to fall. The ocean was boiling with froth as big rollers fought against the receding tide, and the Claro raced past in a torrent.

When the river's depth dropped to three feet, we slid down the steep, sandy bank to the edge. The water was still racing, so I volunteered to test the current before Peter ventured in. I strapped the pack on tight and stepped into the water, which did its best to warn me not to continue. It pulled with wicked strength at my calves, and I couldn't help but glance at the frothy maelstrom offshore where the river seemed hell-bent on dragging me.

I took another step, and now the water was above my knees. It was all I could do to stay upright; going forward was out of the question. I formed a new goal: get back to shore without falling down and drowning in the surf. I leaned into the current and slid my feet in micro steps until I was facing upstream, which gave me a perfect view of the four Europeans calmly fording the river a hundred yards away in ankle-high water. One waved before disappearing into the forest on the other side.

I cursed under my breath. The crafty continentals must have read the park literature.

When I had made it back to shore, we scrambled up the bank and walked to the ford, which was clearly marked with a wooden sign on the far side where the trail snaked into the woods. Peter, who had pulled the park map from the pack, wanted to continue up the beach to an airstrip and then follow it to park headquarters. I argued that the path would be faster since we were already on it.

"Besides," I began, and even though I felt a warning twitch deep in my guts, I couldn't stop myself, "the Europeans did it. The path must be as clear as the autobahn."

In ten minutes we were hopelessly lost. The trail had led through a bog, and though we kept our heading, we couldn't see a path when we came out. When we retraced our steps, the original trail was gone.

"Okay," Peter said. "Let's just walk back to the beach and find the airstrip."

"Good plan," I replied. "You lead."

He set off for what he thought was the beach, but in half an hour we were back at the bog. Or *a* bog. I wouldn't swear it was the same one. So we turned around and stumbled through the trees until Peter stopped short.

"What was that?" he whispered, and I whipped an index finger to my lips so fast I nearly bloodied them. It was a noise unlike anything I had ever heard, yet I knew exactly what it was. The park ranger in San Jose had described it as he showed me a photo of the most ill-tempered animals in the jungle: wild pigs. They make the noise by gnashing their razor-sharp tusks when agitated, and judging by the racket, a bunch of them were having a bad day.

I glanced around at the trees and noticed for the first time that the jungle behemoths weren't really built for climbing. Their trunks were as bare as flower stems until they branched out into the canopy a hundred feet above. That left the ranger's plan. He had said the chances of seeing pigs were slim, but if we did we should stand still as statues until they moved on.

"Of course," he said as he stamped our permits, "it is very hard to stand still while pigs are eating your legs." Then he cackled like a jungle parrot.

I thought of the ranger's joke as the herd moved toward us out of the shadows, and it wasn't nearly as funny this time. About two dozen of the bristly animals, most on the small side but a couple the size of beer kegs, were rooting among the leaves as they ambled ever closer.

Peter and I held our breath as an ugly little outlier came within ten feet before stopping and raising its head. Its nose pulsed as it swept its snout back and forth, and its weak eyes searched the shade for movement. Suddenly it froze and stared right at us, looking for a reason to sound the alarm. We didn't blink. Finally, the pig spun around with a snort and trotted back to the main group. In another minute they had all melted into the forest, which allowed us to breathe and get back to the topic of conversation before we had been so rudely interrupted: Where the hell were we?

There was no way to gauge direction, so we just kept moving in hopes of stumbling across the river, ocean, or trail. For all we knew, however, we were heading for the heart of a thousand square miles of jungle wilderness.

Intent on watching for low-strung spiderwebs, Peter nearly stepped on a big brown snake sleeping in a patch of sun. Preoccupied from that point with what might be lying in my path, I walked face-first into a spider the size of a hen's egg. The web snapped around the back of my skull like a garter and trapped the writhing monster against my forehead. When the echo of my last hysterical scream died away, the jungle was as still as a crypt. Even the insects were holding their breaths.

At dusk, waves of mosquitoes rose from the forest flotsam and sucked the life out of any thought we might have had about stopping for the night.

"I told you we should have just walked up the beach to the airstrip," Peter grumbled, and indeed he had, but I was still impressed that he had the brass to remind me in such a lonely place with no witnesses. He led us back to the bog, and this time we spotted a boot print on a heading perpendicular to ours. We hadn't gone twenty feet before the trail magically appeared between the leaves.

We staggered up to the station's screened-in eating area long after dark. The park ranger, a cook, and the Europeans were sitting around two candles at a long picnic table, eyeing the bit of food they had saved in case we ever arrived. They looked up with surprise as we stumbled scratched and muddy through the door, and one of the women dished the remaining rice and chicken onto two plates.

"Where have you been? We saw you by the river hours ago," she said, and I braced myself for some well-deserved humiliation. But Peter bailed me out.

"Sightseeing," he said as he slid onto the bench, and though we looked as though we'd just gotten back from the budget tour of hell, he stuck to the story. "You see the coolest animals right around dusk."

I could have kissed him.

The rooms were so grim that had it not been for the mosquitoes we'd have slept outside. They were partitioned within a long, narrow, screened-in rectangle of weathered wood, giving the place the look of a giant chicken coop. There were no lights and no sheets for the thin, stained mattresses, and the cockroach-infested latrine was beyond foul. But despite this grim setting, as well as the serious hygiene issues after a long hike in the hot sun, one of the Euro-couples was feeling frisky. They moaned and knocked the bed frame against the paper-thin wall two rooms away.

"Nasty!" Peter spat with the robust disgust he'd displayed after spotting his first zombie in Guatemala.

"Twisted," I agreed.

He shivered. "Makes me want to hurl."

"Yeah, me too," I said. "But it just goes to show you can never under-estimate the power of the human sex drive."

"Huh?"

I looked over, and he was shining his little flashlight at a corner of the top bunk where an ugly spider squatted in the middle of an enormous web.

"Oh, uhhhhhhhh . . ." I yawned and looked at my watch. "Hey, whoa, look at the time! Man, I'm tired. Big day tomorrow. Lights out. See you in the morning."

❦ ❦ ❦

We flew the coop at first light, Peter eager to put some distance between him and the spider and me determined to get out of there before the randy Europeans woke up. We ate granola bars for breakfast as we made our way to the river, where several healthy crocodiles lay like gray logs on the mud flats. Brilliant scarlet flocks of noisy macaws crossed pink patches of sky between trees as tall as football fields, and black-and-yellow toucans whistled from the low branches. It was the monkeys, though, that really stole the show. Spider, capuchin, and squirrel monkeys gamboled through the upper reaches of the forest giants while a troop of howlers squatted in the crotches and roared like the *T. rex* in *Jurassic Park*.

The trails were foot-deep canals filled to the brim with rainy-season mud. With the memory of yesterday's low-hanging spider still fresh in my mind, I didn't pay much attention to my feet. I was stepping over what I thought was a log when Peter screamed, and I glanced down to see the back end of a boa as thick as my calf slither between my legs. It was a good ten feet long and must have weighed fifty pounds, but my enthusiasm got the best of me, and I slid down a creek bank after it.

"What are you *doing*?" Peter yelled as I reached for a tail as thick as my arm.

"I didn't get to see his head," I called, but the thing had evidently seen enough of mine. It hit the water like a torpedo and was out of sight before I'd finished my slide. Good thing too, according to the ranger. The bite hurts like *el diablo*, he said, and people dumb enough to get one usually pick up a nasty infection as well.

"That *was* pretty dumb, Dad," Peter said as we lay on our beds that night. He was shining his little flashlight on the spider.

"Yeah, I guess so." I yawned. "I just got a little excited."

"And what were you thinking when you ticked off those monkeys?"

"I didn't tick off any monkeys!" I retorted, and the beam of light flashed across the ceiling and came to rest on my face.

"Are you serious? They tried to *pee* on us!" The beam jiggled as Peter began to chortle.

I cupped a hand around my face to shield my eyes. "I was just practicing my howler monkey imitation, which was pretty good if I do say so myself." I reached out of the bunk and took a swipe at the flashlight, which he pulled back just far enough to leave my hand flailing in space. "Those monkeys just had to pee, and since they were in the trees above us it just happened to fall in our vicinity. If they'd been mad, they'd have hit you with a turd." I lunged for the light, but Peter rolled to the far side of his bed. "And unless you want a demonstration of *that* bit of monkey behavior, you'd better get that freakin' light out of my eyes."

The room went dark. I walked my hands back across the floor and heaved myself onto my bed. I could hear Peter giggling quietly, but for a long time after the only sound was the hum of insects on the other side of the screen. I was beat from the hike and fading fast, but just as I was drifting off, he spoke again.

"Dad?"

"Hmm?"

"I love you."

I turned my head and stared at the dim outline in the next bunk. It had been a long time since I'd heard those words from Peter, and longer still since I'd deserved them. I wasn't sure I did now, but I wasn't about to quibble.

"I love you too, buddy," I answered, which got me wondering. When was the last time I'd said it? Months? Years?

"Peter?"

"Hmm?"

"I'm really glad you came on this trip."

"Me too." The light flashed back on, but this time he kept the beam above my face.

"Dad?"

"Hmm?"

"You're my best friend."

The light went off, and just before dawn I managed to drift off to sleep.

FOURTEEN

We rocked our hammocks in the shade of a palm and watched the sunlight sparkle on the empty blue expanse of the Pacific Ocean. Our two-bed thatched hut stood a few paces behind us, and the high-tide mark lay a few feet in front, though now, at midday, we were fifty yards from the water.

Empty sand extended in both directions for miles, lined by waving stands of tropical greenery. Frisky seabirds circled and dove just off the coast into water as clear and warm as a baby's bath, and the only sign of life on land was a few hermit crabs scuttling at the forest's edge. Every few seconds, the water reared up into a sparkling green wall, curled, and crashed across the beach in an explosion of sand and foam.

"Eighty-six," Peter intoned.

To call Las Lajas beautiful was an insult. It was the tropical paradise of a million January daydreams. We were the pampered denizens of a postcard.

"Eighty-seven."

The place was cheap, too, just ten dollars a night with access to a concrete bathroom with lukewarm showers. What more could anyone ask for?

"Eighty (yawwwn) eight."

And besides a few other huts, the only structure for miles around was a fifteen-by-fifteen cinder block pillbox from which a middle-aged Japanese-Panamanian named Kenny served fish, fried plantains, and cold beer for a buck and a half. The place was too good to be true.

"Eighty-nine."

So peaceful.

"Ninety!"

So relaxing.

"Niiiiiinety-one."

"Would you knock it off with the freakin' wave count?!"

Peter's shoulders shook so vigorously with suppressed mirth that his whole hammock bucked. He coughed and wheezed for a few seconds before loosing a long, satisfied sigh followed by a deep, cleansing breath.

"Niiiinety-two," he crooned.

This was payback for yesterday. We'd risen at 4:00 a.m. to assure ourselves a spot on the morning ferry from Puerto Jimenez to Golfito, from which we caught a bus to the border. By the time we'd cleared Panamanian customs at Paso Canoas, Peter was asleep on his feet. He had tried to pass out on the ride to David, but I kept shaking him to point out one marvel or another. For instance, instead of being squashed by a thousand chicken-toting Mayans on a rattletrap with suspect brakes, we had our own padded seats in a modern, air-conditioned microbus. No one was standing in the aisle, and everyone (besides us) was dressed for a day at the office. Some of the structures flanking the flawless blacktop road boasted an affluence we hadn't seen since the nicer parts of Mexico.

When we boarded a gleaming first-class coach in David, a couple of matrons in smart gray dresses wrinkled their noses and leaned away from the aisle. We slid into our assigned seats, and I glared at Peter with what I hoped was the same expression. Slumped against the seat back, he made a valiant attempt to ignore me. I leaned closer. After a few seconds he sighed, and his face swung slowly my way.

"What?" he hissed.

"You, sir, are an uncouth vagabond, and it reflects poorly on this country that they allow such riffraff to share a bus with the decent people. I'm afraid I'm going to have to speak with the authorities."

He stared blankly for a few seconds before his face rolled away and his eyelids drooped. I didn't poke him more than half a dozen times after that, but for some reason he was still holding a grudge.

"Niiiiiiiiiinety-three."

There was more than just payback at work here, however. After two months of regimented days, we weren't handling free time well. We'd filled the prior afternoon with three swims, calisthenics, a long jog up the beach, and two hours at Kenny's fish shack. The sun went down at six, and with no electricity we'd gone to bed by eight, only to spend hours tossing and turning on our thin, sandy mattresses. By the time the sun returned at 6:00 a.m., we were raring to go, but it didn't take long to discover that with no school, shopping, cooking, cleaning, or studying, a day in the tropics could be as oppressively long as the night.

We ate some trail mix for breakfast and took a swim. We did pull-ups from a beam in our hut and jogged up the beach. When we returned after our second swim of the morning, it was only 7:30. We were both getting testy.

"How about some push-ups?" I suggested.

"We did those yesterday," Peter said.

"So what?"

"So today's our day off."

"So what the heck else are you going to do if you don't do push-ups?" I demanded as Peter crawled back into his hammock.

"I'm gonna lounge," he said, lacing his hands behind his head.

"Lazy."

"You're lazy!"

"Oh yeah?" I stepped inside the hut, dropped to the cement floor, and began pumping out a set.

"You're not going down all the way," Peter said without even looking.

"Am so!" I gasped.

"Are not. You're doing girl-ups."

"At least I'm doing something," I wheezed as I rolled to my back and checked my watch.

It was 7:35.

I lay there and stared at the ocean through the palm-log doorway. Free time was especially hard on me because unsettling questions rushed in to fill the void. Would our money run out before we got home? And speaking of home, could I do another twenty years on the night shift without hanging myself in the shower? And what about the punk in the hammock? I hadn't checked his homework since Guatemala. Maybe he'd finished it so fast because he wasn't really getting it. Maybe he'd get home and be so far behind that he'd never catch up.

I scrambled to my feet, retrieved a Spanish novel, and tossed it onto Peter's chest.

"Read out loud."

Recognizing the Dad-is-stressed tone, he didn't argue. And he read a chapter so effortlessly that I began to feel a little better. At least he wouldn't be behind in Spanish. I scanned the horizon for something to kill another few minutes. I settled on geography lessons, and I threw in a few bucks to make things interesting.

"I'll bet you ten bucks that you can't name the first continent you would hit if you started swimming away from this beach at a ninety-degree angle," I said, confident that, like myself before I had reviewed the map, he would have no idea that the Pacific Ocean lay directly to our south.

"Give me two chances?" he asked, always angling for a better deal.

"Okay, but if you need both you only get five bucks."

He thought about it for a few seconds before suddenly climbing out of his hammock and ducking inside. He returned with a notebook, from which he tore two scraps of paper. He wrote on one and folded it in half.

"If one of my answers is right I get five dollars," he said. "If both are wrong, I give you ten dollars."

I nodded and he handed me the pen and a scrap of paper.

"Now you write down your answer," he said. "If you're wrong, you owe me an extra ten dollars."

I didn't like the complex turn of this formerly simple contract, and I studied Peter's face for any sign that I was being rolled.

"Has your class ever studied geography?" I asked as I scribbled down *Antarctica*.

"Maybe. I don't remember," he said, and I believed him. With grades like his, how would he?

"Okay, here you go." We exchanged papers and he immediately started chortling.

"What's so funny?" I demanded as I unfolded his scrap.

"I won at least five dollars, but I probably just made fifteen."

"There's no way I lost fifteen," I muttered, but there was no doubt that his answers had put him in the running. Like me, he had written *Antarctica*, but he had also put down *South America*, which appeared on a cocktail-napkin map that he pulled with a flourish from his pack to take a significant enough jog in Peru to lie directly to our south.

"This doesn't count. It's a freakin' napkin."

Peter just laughed. "Pay me the five dollars now, and we'll check a better map when we find one," he said. "But then you'll probably owe me another ten. Or you can just pay me ten now, and we'll call it even."

The kid had been a con artist since the day he could talk. He wasn't quite three when he spotted my grandfather fiddling with a hearing aid at the kitchen table. He pulled his binky from his mouth and crawled into the old man's lap for a better look.

"What's that, Grandpa Eddie?"

"It's a hearing aid."

"Can I see it?"

"Well, no," my grandfather said gently. "This is just for people who have trouble hearing."

"What?" Peter said, and my grandfather repeated it.

"What?" Peter said again, and the adults finally caught on to the toddler's scam.

I nodded to the doorway and lay back in my hammock.

"My money's in the top of the pack," I said. "Go get your ten bucks."

There was no question the kid was sharp. He just hadn't ever been challenged to work to his capabilities. I wondered what drifting around Central America for two months was going to do to his newfound discipline. Maybe we should have done the trip backward with the schoolwork at the end.

Suddenly twitchy with angst, I drilled Peter in Spanish until we were both close to nodding off.

It was 8:30.

We went for another swim, had a nap, and took a long walk to the fish shack, which was a great place to kill time because Kenny was such a slow cook. I made a supreme effort not to check my watch, but when I

135

finally did as we walked back to our hut, I was positive it was at least 1:00 p.m. Peter insisted it was past 2:00, and I won my first wager of the trip.

It was 11:00 a.m.

By noon we were bickering over whether to head back to Kenny's for our second lunch of the day or wait until 4:00 p.m. for the first of two dinners, and Peter started counting waves. I was swaying in my hammock, watching the sea and wondering how we were going to make it a week without a murder when the answer sashayed over in a tiny black bikini. She was a dark-haired stunner, at least six feet tall, with the smile of a toothpaste model and a figure made for that little suit. She was carrying two ice-cold Panama beers, one of which she handed to me.

"I'm Monique," she said and held out her hand, which I clumsily took as I wrestled my way out of the hammock.

"Kirk," I croaked. My throat was suddenly as dry as sun-baked sand. "And that's my son, Peter."

She stepped with the grace of a doe around to Peter's hammock while I drained half my bottle in one long pull.

"Do you drink beer, Peter?" she asked, and in reply he snatched the bottle with a hearty "Thanks!" and took a long swig.

Monique laughed.

"Excellent," she said with an accent I couldn't place. "Would you boys like to play some cards?"

It was an innocent invitation from a friendly fellow traveler, and I tried hard to convince myself that there could be no harm in it, which might have been true had our hostess been a homely gal who packed a muumuu like a kielbasa. But Monique was gorgeous, lithe, and nearly naked, and I knew darned well it was a bad idea.

So I said, "Sure!" My mouth had been jarred loose from my conscience when that bikini sideswiped my eyes.

"Follow me," she said and turned to lead the way through the trees. My wobbly knees nearly gave out on the first step, but I righted myself on the post just as Peter hustled past. So compelling was the view from behind our gorgeous guide that I didn't notice another woman sitting at a table until we were twenty feet away.

Hilary was a slim six-foot blonde, quieter than her friend but nearly as pretty. The gals were in their early twenties and had been traveling through Central America for a month. They were from Germany but had studied in London, which gave their English an exotic lilt.

The fetching *fräuleins* had a cooler full of beer, which we finished during the next couple of hours of blackjack. I was vaguely aware of Peter downing one bottle and grabbing another, but I have to admit I fell down on the parenting job that afternoon. It was all I could do to remember not to hit twenty-one.

Peter took an instant liking to the gals and seemed enchanted by their personalities. I envied him that innocence, which most guys lose forever at about his age but which he evidently still possessed. *Enjoy it, buddy,* I thought more than once. *It won't be long before the hormones kick your privates up around your brainpan.* They weren't there yet, however. He laughed and joked and was the life of the party, and the women were charmed.

Monique and Hilary taught Peter to open beer bottles with a plastic lighter and to blow perfect smoke rings, which would liven up his "What I Learned in Central America" essay when he got back to school. Monique also taught him the secret of traveling light, though only after some merciless teasing about the immensity of his backpack.

"Take a daypack, and you will never bring more than you really need," she said, indicating the dimensions of hers with quick motions of her hands. "I have two shirts, some underwear, shorts, a skirt, this swimsuit, and one pair of pants," she added, but I wasn't as impressed with the size of her pack as she was. If the rest of her clothes were as skimpy as her bikini, she could have gotten by with a lunch box.

The gals were savvy travelers, having spent months on previous trips to different parts of South America. They had learned that the most effective strategy for discouraging local Romeos was to never appear unattached, which was where Peter and I came in. The gals had scoped us out the day before and figured that hanging with a giant and his strapping son was as good as hiring bodyguards. It worked too. A couple of the young bucks who cleaned the grounds had been pestering the women since their arrival two days before, but with us around the men kept their distance.

I wasn't complaining about our role, which took some of the tawdriness out of the way we were spending the afternoon. We were protectors, which seemed noble regardless of what was running through my head. When the beer ran out, the gals raced back to their hut and retrieved a bag of pasta and a can of tuna, which they whipped into a hearty dish in the communal kitchen and served to us at the picnic table. It was memorable day, but it came with a price.

I spent the last hour of daylight fidgeting in my hammock before crawling into bed for a fruitless attempt to sleep. I tried counting sheep for a while but had to stop when they started coming over the fence in black bikinis. It was a long night.

The gals stopped by in the morning to invite us to Kenny's for breakfast, and when we split up again I was as grumpy as a bear. I felt like a chocoholic at a diet camp, and around every corner was a plate of brownies I couldn't have. And this addict had been sugar-free for more than two months.

Back at the hut I taunted Peter for bailing out on his pull-ups, which he did only because a wasp the size of a sparrow had tried to set down on his eyeball. I drilled him relentlessly in Spanish later as we walked five miles to town to buy more supplies, and I badgered him over every error.

"Why are you being such a butthead?" he finally demanded as we waited for a cab back to the beach.

I sat down on the curb and twisted the tops off two cold drinks. I handed him one and struggled to come up with an explanation that a kid could understand. But at its core, I realized, this was really just the same old story: Something had me stirred up, and Peter was taking the fallout. I wound up apologizing yet again and promised to cheer up. I also made a silent resolution to steer clear of the women.

When we got back, it was only noon, so we worked out, went for a swim, and climbed into our hammocks. Monique and Hilary showed up soon after—wearing shorts and tank tops, thank goodness, but still pretty enough to tempt a monk.

"Do you want to jog up the beach to the river?" Monique asked, and I thought, *Well, that's a kind offer, and I do appreciate it, but I could do without the testosterone overdose this afternoon, so I'm afraid we'll have to decline and ask you to take those perfect brown thighs on up the beach without us.*

But my feeble mouth croaked, "Sure," and my treacherous legs slid off the hammock, and before I knew it I was stumbling up the beach after the brownies.

Another day went by in a blur of beer and sun and skin, and as I crawled into my bunk to face another restless night I knew we had to get out of there. I didn't know what Peter would think. He had been looking forward to the beach for months, and they didn't come any prettier than this one. I spent half an hour laying out a careful rhetorical strategy, and if all else failed I would bribe him. I cleared my throat.

"Peter. You still awake?"

"Yeah," he replied lethargically.

"What would you think about cutting the beach time short and moving on?"

I heard his sheets rustle as he slid to the edge of his bed. His silhouette filled the doorway.

"What are you doing?"

"I'm getting packed!"

Maybe Peter hadn't understood exactly why I'd been so grumpy, but he knew my mood had something to do with the location. He'd had enough.

He left the hut and returned a minute later with our laundry, which had been strung along a cord under the porch. I lit a candle, and a few minutes later our packs were full and standing at attention by the door.

We were up at dawn, but we wanted to say good-bye to the gals, so we waited on our hammocks until we saw them heading for the bathrooms. We shouldered our packs and walked over to wait outside, and Monique's face fell the second she emerged. There was a dance in a nearby town in a couple of days, and she was hoping we would go.

"Oh, please, please stay," she pleaded in a tone that spiked my blood sugar. "I was going to teach you how to samba today."

She extended her willowy arms and curled both index fingers in a seductive invitation to come hither. Her thighs flexed and her hips swiveled, and the lethal breeze of a dodged bullet swished past my ear.

Peter and I gave the girls a hug, grabbed our packs, and fled up the dirt road away from what, in my opinion, had been the most dangerous portion of our trip.

FIFTEEN

I barely heard the door slam, so loud was the pounding of blood in my ears. I was surrounded by a dozen grim faces and two smirking ones, which belonged to the camera thieves I'd chased into this flophouse in Chitré. We were still far from the End of the Road, but it looked like the end of mine. I guess the babes weren't the most dangerous part of the trip after all . . .

. . . Nah, they were the worst. Still, this was plenty bad, and I was kicking myself for trusting the hoodlums who had led me into the trap.

The trouble was, Panamanians had been so honest since we'd left Las Lajas that my suspicious nature began to seem like just another character flaw. It had started with the driver of a pickup who gave us a ride from the beach to town. He wouldn't take a dime for it, which left me so dumbfounded I forgot to haggle with the cabbie over a fare to the highway. But instead of taking advantage, the guy charged the same as the locals paid: two bucks.

"That's weird," I said to Peter as we dragged our packs to the shoulder to wait for the bus.

"What's weird?"

"In twenty years of travels south of the border, I've never seen a local pass up a chance to gouge a tourist, and it just happened twice in ten minutes. These guys are honest."

Peter shook his head. "Nah, they just feel sorry for you. You look like a hobo."

His theory had merit, but I still thought more of mine: the Las Lajas guys hadn't yet been jaded by hordes of foreign visitors. Things would be different in a few years, and they probably already were in Panama's bigger towns.

Peter sat against his pack and cradled his new best friend, a half-gallon plastic jug that the girls had given him. They'd been appalled that he was taking antibiotics for something as common as pimples, insisting that all he needed was a lot of water and sun. Peter jumped on the band-wagon with both feet, which was remarkable because he had never before cared about how he looked. Maybe those little swimsuits had made an impression after all.

He stood up and wandered into the tall grass that lined the highway. The downside of his water regime was that he had to pee all the time, and I was worried about the bus rides ahead.

"You'd better get yourself an empty bottle in case the buses don't have bathrooms," I said when he returned.

"Naw, I can hold it. I'm just going a lot because Monique said that's how you clean the system." He took another long swig. "That and sweating."

He was in luck there. It wasn't even 8:00 a.m. but it was already ninety degrees, and our shirts were soaked. We stewed in the full sun because the only shade was too far from the road, and by the time the bus arrived even our pants were wet.

The passengers shrank from the aisle as they watched us board. We took seats near the back, where I immediately pinched a piece of Peter's threadbare T-shirt between my thumb and forefinger.

"Just look at you!" I said in mock disgust, and I gave the shirt a little shake. "It speaks ill of this country that it lets such vermin on its buses with the decent pe—Hey!"

Peter pushed both forefingers into his cheeks, and a mouthful of lukewarm water splashed into my lap. He had meant to let loose only a dollop but started laughing and hit me with the whole tepid slop. As he doubled over to catch his breath and I brushed at the growing stain on my pants, a well-dressed older woman two seats up and across the aisle twisted around to see what was going on.

"Great," her eyes said. "Now the old reprobate has wet himself."

I could feel the riders relax when we rose to leave at the turnoff for Boca Chica, and I could imagine their clucks of disdain as Peter went for his zipper and dashed into the weeds before the bus pulled away.

"Hey," I called. "Couldn't you at least wait a few seconds for the old ladies to leave?"

"They aren't watching me," he yelled without turning. "They're all looking at your pee stain."

I left him to his guffawing and wandered over to a cabbie who had taken a gamble to drive out from town to meet our bus. If we hadn't gotten off, he'd have been skunked, but now he stood to hit the jackpot. Boca Chica was probably fifteen miles away, which was too far to walk in the heat even without a sixty-pound pack, so I was stunned when he only asked for five dollars.

"See?" Peter said as we scrambled into the backseat. "Your hobo-ness is like a discount card. And your stain probably saved us an extra 10 percent."

He giggled like an eight-year-old for the whole ride. Our escape from Temptation Island had him in a fine mood, and I have to admit it was contagious. I didn't even blink later that day when I realized that the six-dollar lobster that had enticed us to Boca Brava cost twenty-three once we figured in costs for bus, cab, and ferry. I just reminded myself how little money we had spent in Las Lajas and how much I had saved by leaving early. Marriage counseling isn't cheap.

While we were waiting for our meals, the sounds of a fiesta drifted up from the docks. A minute later, five sunburned men staggered over to a nearby table and slammed down two liquor bottles that were perilously close to being empty.

The noisiest of the group called for us to join in. They had been out on a boat for two weeks and had just returned with a hold full of snapper. They were celebrating and wanted us to be their guests.

My eyes met Peter's, and we read each other's minds. It wasn't that a party didn't sound fun, but what would happen when the bill arrived? I couldn't see that gang picking through the check like old ladies at a luncheon—"Now Carlos dear, you had seventeen beers; and Paco, you and Armando shared five lobsters, thirty-seven clams, and three bottles of rum. You owe . . ."—and I didn't want to split it seven ways. It was also not inconceivable that they might expect the gringo to foot the bill because anyone who had ever watched an episode of *Dallas* knew all Americans were rolling in dough.

We thanked them and returned our attention to the important task of folding our paper napkins into the smallest possible squares. The waitress came and went, but she was back in a heartbeat with two more bottles of booze and six beers, one of which she set in front of me.

"Join us, amigos," the man yelled, and the others stood and rearranged chairs to make a space.

"Here we go," I muttered, smiling weakly as we made our way to their table.

They poured me a shot of rum and ordered Peter a Coke. There was another round of beers and some appetizers that they insisted we share. By the time our dinner arrived I was so worked up I had no appetite, but I wolfed it down so we could get out of there before the revelers ordered something else. I gave the waitress fifteen bucks for our bill and tried to hand another ten to our host.

Carlos frowned at the money and then dismissed it with a wave.

"This is our party, my friend, and you are our guests. Won't you stay and help us celebrate?"

Blood rushed to my face and burned my ears. I felt like the suspicious, small-spirited piker that I was, and I didn't feel worthy to drink with such generous men. I scuttled out of the dining area after Peter and climbed down onto the path, which was harder than it sounds because it was at least a six-inch drop and I had shrunk to two and a half inches.

After that I stopped trying to analyze the motives of Panamanians, who seemed the friendliest strangers I'd ever encountered. When we left Boca Brava the next morning, I gave the waitress money to buy a round for the fishermen when they came back in. I didn't worry that she might just keep it for herself. I was pretty sure a thought like that had never crossed her mind.

We caught a bus to Chitré, and my new attitude painted everything in cheerful hues. The farmland we traversed wasn't dull; it was impossibly green with crops laid out in impeccably straight rows. I took the disdainful looks of the other riders as a sign of their breeding and sophistication. I needed a shave, we both needed haircuts, and our clothes carried that slightly sour smell of laundry done by hand in a bathroom sink—and that was before we had sweated them through while waiting for the bus. Of course those fine people wrinkled their noses in disgust. We were pigs!

But not for long, by jiminy! After checking into our hotel, we showered and changed and headed back outside with a bag of dirty clothes, determined to raise our standards to those of our new favorite country.

We left the laundry with an old woman who promised to have it washed and dried in two hours for three dollars. Across the street was a beauty shop, which offered haircuts for the same price. I couldn't pass up that kind of bargain, and besides, as I told Peter on the walk over, he could stand a little beautifying.

"If they serve your kind, I'm walking out of there," he retorted, but he stayed. How could he not, with two cute young women in spotless uniforms of pink and white cotton waving us into the chairs? *Beautiful gals*, I thought reflexively, but were they really? Could every female in this country be truly attractive, or had I just been away from my wife too long? I studied the gals in the mirror as they chopped off two months' of hair and decided that they probably weren't natural beauties. What set them apart was their immaculate grooming and stylish mode of dress. Take away the makeup, drop them into a pair of sweatpants, and add a case of bed-head, and you'd have typical American twenty-somethings.

But even if all the gals down here were getting a little lift from their hygiene, they looked great, and so did their charming town. I marveled at how the well-fed men in their business suits could hustle through the humid heat without so much as a sheen on their brows, while we were soaked within a minute of stepping outside. Incredible people, these Panamanians!

Surely in such a place there was no harm in using my camera. I had never carried it in Latin American cities for the same reason I didn't bring a hunk of bloody liver when I swam in the ocean, but things felt different in Chitré. Besides, we were enjoying a delightful Independence Day parade from the safety of a hotel balcony, well above the crowds lining the street. I wanted some photos of the girls in their nineteenth-century dresses, so I ignored my suspicions and retrieved the camera from our room. It wasn't two minutes before the sharks began to circle.

My first hint of trouble was that the do-rag dudes leaning on the rail a few feet away weren't watching the parade. But they walked up smiling and chattering, and even though it was a hard-to-follow mix of unschooled Spanish and Caribbean gutter slang, the tone was friendly. I caught enough words to figure out that they were from Colón, a crime-ridden hole across the isthmus that every guidebook warned travelers to avoid, but they didn't seem menacing there on the balcony.

When one asked if he could take a picture, he set off a spirited discussion in my head. A new voice that I didn't recognize was as calm and soothing as a lullaby. She told me not to worry, that things would be fine because everyone we had met so far in Panama had been as helpful as Boy Scouts. The old voice was as jarring as a fire bell, and she played on a loop at an ever-increasing volume in a fruitless attempt to drown out the interloper. "Don't do it! Don't do it! *Don't do it!*"

But I did it. The guy snapped one picture of his buddy flashing gang signs, and then both took off running down the stairs.

"I told you so," said the old voice as I raced down the stairwell and onto the street. The new one had flown back to whatever fairyland she had come from, leaving the angry harpy to harangue me as I chased the gangsters.

I dodged through the crowd for two blocks with Peter on my heels. Just as I got close enough to reach for the guy in back, the pair took a hard right into a flophouse. They fled across the foyer, ducked into a room, and tried to shut the door, but I bulled my way in after them. The door slammed behind me, and the scene that congealed as my eyes adjusted to the room's dim light left the old scold nearly speechless.

"Uh-oh," she squeaked before flying off to fairyland with the sweet-voiced meddler.

Blocking the door of the twelve-by-twelve rent-a-slum was the biggest human I'd seen since we had left the United States. He was at least six foot eight, and though there didn't appear to be a dollop of fat on him, he looked to be an easy 280 pounds. His meaty shoulders reached from one doorframe to the other, and his close-cropped head drooped slightly in a manner suggesting someone accustomed to bumping it on things. His muscular neck bulged out beyond his ears.

The others were sprawled across the mattress or leaning shoulder-to-shoulder against the plaster walls. The only sound was the squeak of the bedsprings as one man eased himself to his feet.

I wondered if Peter would have the presence of mind to lead a cop to the room. Maybe eventually, I decided, but not soon enough to do me any good. I was on my own, and since there was no fighting my way out of that sardine can, I forced a smile and started talking fast.

"Friends," I shouted in Spanish as the sweat began to run off my upper lip. "I have come from the United States to take your picture! Let's go outside now so I can get a good one."

Nobody moved, though I saw a few eyes flash toward the big guy. I stole a glance and felt a wild pang of hope as his giant face lit up. When he snatched the camera from the thief and began shooing everyone out the door, I went limp with relief.

Peter was in the foyer looking worried when I shuffled out in the middle of the line.

"Wait on the street," I mouthed before turning to Shaquille O'Neal's Panamanian cousin, who was fiddling with the camera buttons and looking through the wrong side of the viewfinder. He somehow managed to snap a photo of me and some of his relatives, but he showed no inclination to return the camera.

"But you are not in the picture, my friend," I said with mock concern as I eased the camera out of his massive hand. "Stand over there and I will take your picture."

He did, but I didn't. I faked the photo as I was backing through the foyer, ducked out the front door, and followed Peter in an all-out sprint for our hotel.

He started in on me the second I locked the door to our room. "I told you it was a bad idea to come to this town."

"You said it sounded boring. That wasn't boring, was it?"

"Well, you owe me a hundred dollars for being stupid."

I chuckled mirthlessly. "The deal was I that can't cuss or lose my temper. I never said anything about being stupid." *I couldn't afford that bill*, I thought as I flopped onto my bed, closed my eyes, and rubbed my temples, but Peter continued pacing around the room.

"So what are we supposed to do now, huh? You fixed it so we can't even go outside to watch the stupid parade we came here to see."

"If you want to watch the parade, we can go back to the balc—"

"Screw the parade! It's lame! This whole town is lame!"

My jaw clenched. The past week had been blissfully gripe-free, and I wasn't about to let Peter get started down that road again. I looked up, but my retort died in my throat as I watched him swipe his eyes with the heels of his hands.

"Hey, what's wrong?" I sat up and slid my legs toward the edge of the bed, but he backed away.

"I thought you were dead!" he barked hoarsely and stormed into the bathroom.

For half a minute, all I could do was stare at the door and listen to the muffled splash of water as Peter washed his face. I'd been thinking about how scared I'd been locked in that room with the Crips, but I'd never stopped to consider the hell he must have faced on the other side of the door.

The peal of trumpets wafted in from the street on the hotel's far side. The music faded as the musicians marched away, replaced by the rhythmic pounding of a dozen drums. The water stopped, and Peter stepped out, red-faced but in control.

"That was dumber than chasing a boa into a creek," he said, to which I nodded agreeably. "And you've made a ton of other bad decisions this trip."

I folded my arms and frowned with concentration, but I couldn't say much in my defense. I took the Fifth.

"It's my turn to drive." He walked to the desk by the door, picked up the Central American guidebook, and quickly flipped through the pages—too quickly, I realized later. He knew exactly what he was looking for.

♥ ♥ ♥

The Caribbean swells were monsters outside the shelter of the islands. Just out of curiosity, I raised my paddle from the bottom of a trough and tried to slap the top of an average roller. Not even close.

Peter had the seat in the front of our two-man sea kayak as befitted his new position of leadership, and I could see the curl of an approaching breaker several feet above his head.

"Captain?"

"Don't bug me, private," he snapped. "I'm navigating."

We surfed up the face, teetered on the ridge for a sickening split-second, and slid down the back into another trough. From the top I had spotted a sheltered cove of an island not more than a quarter mile off. It was a few degrees to the right of Peter's back, which I couldn't help but notice was as bare as the day he was born—as was mine.

"You didn't happen to stash a couple of life preservers under your seat before we shoved off, did you, sir?" This set off a spirited discussion about the chain of command, which deteriorated quickly as a wave spun us around and dropped us backward off its face.

The next one broke across my back and shoved us so deep that I thought we had flipped. But we popped up like a cork, still upright, and when I'd finished coughing up seawater, I gasped, "That's it! I'm taking command!"

The recriminations were instant and fierce. Insults were lobbed and threats leveled, including a particularly ugly promise to hack off someone's head with a clamshell. But we made it to the cove, and the unpleasantness was soon forgotten. It's hard to stay mad in paradise.

Peter couldn't have picked a prettier destination than Bocas del Toro. It was also one of the most historically rich areas in Central America. Columbus had fallen hard for the archipelago in 1502, and he named three sites after himself: Isla Colón (Columbus Island), Isla Cristobal (Christopher Island), and Bahía Almirante (Admiral Bay). It had been a haven for pirates in the 1600s, including Sir Francis Drake and Henry Morgan, and local legend said a fortune in buried booty was still waiting for a lucky prospector.

But I knew history wasn't why Peter had picked Bocas, and it was clear that the amenities hadn't drawn him there. The main island, Colón (no relation to the slum down the coast), had the typical ramshackle look of the rest of Central America's Caribbean coast, though it had a few nice restaurants and hotels sprinkled amid an older mishmash along the sandy main drag. We took an eight-dollar room in a shanty hammered together from tin and weathered boards where ants came streaming out of the floor every morning on designated pathways that thankfully did not traverse our beds.

Peter had had one thing in mind when he picked Bocas, which I learned soon after we paddled back to the dock. As we strolled to our room, I couldn't help but notice his longing stares at a sign touting scuba lessons. I tried, but he got me in an arm-bar and forced me to turn my head.

"You're the accountant," I said. "You know we don't have enough money for that."

"I know," he replied, but before he let me go, he made me run through some calculations. We had about twenty-five hundred dollars left to last five weeks, which sounded like a lot more than it was. To be safe, we had to set aside a thousand dollars for the three-thousand-mile drive from Tapachula, Mexico, to Salt Lake City. Travel back to our car would eat up a couple hundred, and meals and hotels for thirty-five days could take another thousand. That left three hundred dollars for every other unforeseen expense that came along. The lessons were two hundred bucks apiece.

Peter dropped my arm with a sigh. We turned to head back to our room, but before we'd gone five feet a voice exploded from the dive shack: "Vait! Vait!"

Out of the doorway scampered a short, rotund sausage of an Austrian who had miraculously stuffed himself into Speedo.

"You vant scuba, no?" he said, and when I told him we couldn't afford it, he scoffed. "Vhere you stay?"

I told him the name of our dump, and he frowned with disappointment. He stared up and down the empty street, glanced back at his empty shop, and turned to me.

"I have special: forty-five dollars. But ees introduction only. No certificate."

When I said okay, Peter did a perfect imitation of a leaky balloon, releasing his breath in a noisy burst as he sprung toward the sky.

We were geared up in minutes, and Helmut led us toward water so murky I could only see a foot of the rope that moored the floating dock to the bottom of the bay.

"You smart guys, no? You hear vhat I say? Breathe vith deees one."

He popped a rubber thingamajig into my mouth.

"Poosh deees to empty vest unt go down. Poosh deees to fill vest unt go up."

He repeated his instructions to Peter, gave a little wave, and jumped off the dock. I was a second behind Peter, but when the water closed above my head I was alone in the murk. I drifted toward the bottom like shark chum, squeezing my nose and blowing in a frantic attempt to keep my eardrums from bursting until the pain overwhelmed all thought. I mashed the Up button and rocketed to the surface, which I breached like a gray whale just inches from the edge of the floating dock. That would have hurt.

I figured I'd gotten my forty-five bucks' worth, and I was about to climb out when the other two appeared behind me. Helmut again showed me how to use the vest to equalize my weight, and he stayed closer this time. He led us slowly downward, stopping every few feet to wait for my thumbs-up. I could make out Peter floating patiently a few feet away, so even though it felt like someone's thumbs were jammed in my ears, I gave the signal and headed deeper.

We stopped at twenty feet and again at thirty, where I started seeing bright flashes timed to the throbbing in my head. Peter swam close and raised a questioning thumb, so I forced my eyes wide in a pantomime of delight and gave him two thumbs back. What did I really need eardrums for anyway?

At thirty-five feet I could feel that something was about to blow, and I looked forward to the soothing rush of seawater that would soon fill my skull. But there would be no relief because just then we reached the floor, where I drifted in a limbo of agony amid the silty detritus. I remember a metal chair and a few beer cans, as well as plastic bags that swayed with the current like bottom-feeding jelly fish. Something bigger lay off to my left, a mud-covered lump that could have been a dolphin or an oil drum or some other poor sap who couldn't clear his ears.

By the time we heaved ourselves out atop the dock, I'd have paid forty-five bucks not to go back in, and I was sad that after all these months of dreaming, Peter's scuba experience had been such a debacle. I spat out my regulator, yanked off my mask and fins, and carried the equipment into the dive shack. Peter didn't say a thing as he stowed his gear, and he looked dazed as we walked out to the street. I felt horrible.

"Peter," I began. "I just . . ." But words failed me. What could I say?

"I know, Dad. I know," he answered solemnly. He took a deep breath and let it out in a long stream. "That was the coolest ten minutes of my life."

SIXTEEN

I had traced a finger along the map's winding lines a hundred times. The spiderweb in Mexico collapsed into a few thin threads as I slid through Central America until, at last, a single black squiggle snaked its way east out of Panama City. Somewhere near the Colombian border, amid a confusion of rivers large and small, the line disappeared.

The stretch between the End of the Road in Yaviza and a pueblo a hundred miles away in Colombia is called the Darién Gap, and I was beguiled by the audacity of an expanse so wild it could defy twentieth-century progress. Its swamps, rivers, mountains, and the most pristine jungle outside of the Amazon were an engineer's nightmare, and by the time the brainiacs figured out how to build a road, the Panamanians didn't want it. They figured they had enough trouble with Colombian rebels and drug-runners without improving their access.

The Gap had played the flame to many a moth over the centuries, and as we rolled across the Panama Canal on the Bridge of the Americas, my heart was fluttering like the insect's dusty wings. We were just a couple of hundred miles away.

When we got off the bus at Panama City's Albrook terminal, we raced to the ticket booth, smiled at the bored young attendant, and asked for two first-class tickets on the afternoon bus to Yaviza.

The gal's sleepy eyes widened with amusement, and she stifled a little laugh. She was a typical Panamanian beauty, but that pretty face masked the mind of a psychopath.

"The bus runs once a week," she said and then clammed up. She met my look of horror with a toothy grin that broadened with each passing second.

I opened my mouth, but nothing came out. Her pretty eyes twinkled.

Finally, Peter stepped up to ask when the next bus left, and her face relaxed into its normal, bored expression.

"Tomorrow at three a.m.," she said, suddenly all business. "Be here by two thirty. That will be twenty-eight dollars."

We were so relieved that we weren't fazed by the exorbitant fare. In fact, the more we thought about the price, the more convinced we became that we were in for the ride of our lives.

"It only cost ten dollars to get all the way here from David on the nicest bus I've ever seen," Peter said as we walked away with our tickets. "This one must have movies and meals. I'll bet the seats fold out into beds."

The glory of the Albrook terminal encouraged such lavish specula-tion. It was the Taj Majal of bus stations, accommodating sixteen hun-dred trips a day, and it was bigger and more modern than a lot of US airports. Every bus we passed was a gleaming paragon of the species, so a fourteen-dollar bus must be some bus indeed. We could hardly wait.

Panama City's towering skyline rivaled Miami's, and the capital was in the midst of a construction boom that would soon double its impressive collection of glass-and-steel high-rises. We spent the day hitting the tour-ist high points—the ruins of Old Panama, the locks on the famous canal, a sanctuary for giant monkey-eating harpy eagles—then turned in early. We had to catch a cab by 2:00 a.m., which meant we ought to rise by 1:45.

When the front desk made the wake-up call, we were already up and showered. We weren't about to take the chance of missing the week's only bus, so we never really slept. It was no big deal, though. We could have a long nap on our ride's heated water beds.

"I might skip the bed and go right for the hot tub," I told Peter as we waited for the taxi.

"I don't know," he said skeptically. "You might want to let the giant breakfast settle before you get in the water."

"Excellent point! Okay, nap first, then hot tub."

The cab dropped us at Albrook at two thirty. We immediately took note of the cozy lounges at each modern gate, from which passengers could gaze through wall-high glass at their sparkling coach. Our gate was at the far end of the terminal, a fitting spot for a bus to the End of the Road, and we walked fast so we could enjoy a few minutes of awestruck viewing before we boarded.

"Maybe we should put on our sunglasses so the gleam doesn't hurt our eyes," Peter suggested as we neared the end of the terminal, and I clapped him on the back.

"Always thinking!"

We slipped on our glasses and trotted the last few feet, then skidded to a stop so abrupt you'd have thought we'd been Tasered. Our gate didn't have a lounge, and what we could see through a grease-streaked window in the dented aluminum exit door wasn't sparkling. Squatting in the feeble halo of a single yellow bulb was a battered 1950s school bus. Half of its windows were missing their glass, and its battered door hung askew on long-stripped hinges.

We stared slack-jawed from the beater bus to the fourteen-dollar tickets in our trembling hands. There had to be some mistake. We pushed through the door and approached a young man who was frowning at the bald spots on the vehicle's back tires.

"Is this the bus to Yaviza?" I asked, and I winced as he confirmed the bad news. It got worse.

"Among many other places," he continued. "Sit toward the back if you are going to be with us all twelve hours."

I sucked a gnat into my windpipe and doubled over in a coughing fit. Peter whacked me on the back a few times, but I suspected from the vigor of the blows that he was just working off some frustration. By the time I could breathe again, the young man had boarded the bus. We peered past the broken door at the dented metal steps, on which not a scrap of the original rubber safety mats remained. The driver's seat was crisscrossed with duct tape, only a few small triangles of the Naugahyde cover showing through.

We climbed the stairs and handed our tickets to the attendant, who had taken the seat closest to the door.

"Why twelve hours?" I croaked. "It's only a few hundred kilometers."

He chuckled. "A few hundred kilometers of bad road, my friend." He nodded toward the back, and we trudged dejectedly down the narrow aisle.

The torn seats were spaced for the kindergartners the bus had carried a few decades before. Peter and I wedged ourselves in, but we had to point our knees toward the window. Our bench was missing its foam pad and plastic cover, and we balanced uncomfortably on a thick metal bar. Mosquitoes droned in the darkness as we waited for the driver to join us on board.

The bus rode worse than it looked. It listed to the right, and even at fifteen miles per hour it bounced like the mechanical horse outside Kmart. Instead of taking the freeway, the driver stuck to surface streets, which funneled us into an infamous district known as San Miguelito. The high-crime slum had had a chip on its shoulder about the United States since being bombed during the 1989 invasion, and the guidebook warned tourists to steer clear even during the day. But the driver apparently hadn't read that chapter. He lurched to the side of the road every couple of blocks to pick up clusters of drunks, and soon the bus was so jammed that a woman in the aisle had to rest her mammoth fanny on my shoulder to keep from falling over.

The air was a foul mix of booze, sweat, and cheap cologne, and for the first time in three months, Peter's spirit broke. He looked helplessly at the smelly mob around us, glanced at his watch, and did the awful math. He rested his arms on the seat back in front of him and buried his face.

I kept mine turned toward the window. There was nothing to see once we left the city, but the rush of outside air diluted the cabin stench from toxic to merely disgusting. After a while, however, I became distracted by a shaft of light waving low on the horizon. Whenever it vanished behind the trees, I kept my eyes locked on the spot until it reappeared, always a little bigger and brighter.

For reasons I couldn't articulate, the light made me hopeful, and I felt a pang of disappointment when the bus turned left and the beam swung out of view. There was an inky wall outside my window now, with nothing to distract from the misery on the inside.

I tried, though. I closed my eyes and thought about what kind of light could be out there so far from the city. *Probably too remote for a factory, unless they make explosives.* I was dying to check my watch, but I forced my mind back to the light. *Yeah, it could be a fireworks factory or a military base.* My neighbor in the aisle hiked her butt higher onto my neck. *But I thought I read that Panama had decentralized its military, so it's probably a fireworks factory or some other place that needs a lot of buffer like . . . like . . .*

"Peter, wake up!"

I shook him, and his head bounced off the seat back, but he came up smiling because my shouts were granting his fondest wish: "We're getting out of here!"

That friendly light was Tocumen International Airport, and if we could just get off the bus before it went too far, we could walk there and rent a car.

"Get up! Get up," I yelled, but Peter couldn't move unless I did, and I couldn't stand with that eighty-pound ass on my shoulder. There was no time for niceties, and even if there were, to whom would I have addressed them? All I saw when I turned my head was a mountain of buttocks spilling out of a molehill of stretch pants, so I wrestled it into the aisle, dodged a swinging handbag from the owner, and yanked Peter to his feet. I dragged my knapsack off the luggage rack and dove into the mosh pit.

The battle to the front was like a cage match with fifty inebriated tag teams. We were elbowed, pinched, punched, kneed, and head-butted as we pushed past and climbed over the crowd. It was dark, but I'm pretty sure I broke my lifelong rule against hitting women.

"Stop the bus. We're getting off!" I screamed as I shoved my head through the final pack of wrestlers. The driver hauled the bus onto the grassy shoulder and opened the door, but he and the attendant never stopped trying to stop us as we scrambled down the steps. "We aren't there yet," they hollered, but we just strolled off into the sweet night air without a backward glance.

Our unexpected escape left us giddy, and we chattered excitedly as we walked along the deserted road. Even if it meant living on stale tortillas for a week or two, it was worth it to get off that stench bucket.

"And I thought you smelled bad," Peter said. "I owe you an apology."

♥ ♥ ♥

Dawn broke through the windshield of a sweet-smelling, late-model, compact sedan whose hi-fi stereo had no trouble drowning out the rush of refrigerated air that poured from the shiny dash.

We sped along a fine paved road for an hour, making such good time that we figured we would make it to Yaviza by 9:00 a.m. Why the bus needed twelve hours for such a short trip I could not explain, but we had time to burn. When we spotted a sign promising home-cooked meals, I hit the brakes.

The restaurant's single table sat on a patio close to a concrete staircase, on which the proprietress sat to watch us eat our eggs and beef.

"It's good," I said politely, figuring that would satisfy her, and she would wander back to the kitchen. But she just sat there, watching.

"Your son is very handsome," she said out of the blue, and I smiled and nodded and returned to my eggs. No sense starting an argument with a farsighted stranger.

She scurried up the stairs and returned a minute later with a teenage girl in tow, and they both sat down to stare at Peter. I sighed with sincere sympathy. The poor things must not have seen many guys without machete scars out here in Panama's outback.

We finished our food and hurried to the car, pursued by the mother, who insisted that we return for dinner. We could stay the night in their spare bedroom if it got too late, she offered, almost pleading.

I was still shaking my head five minutes down the road. What the heck was that all about?

We drove a while through rolling hills that the narrow road matched contour for contour, and the converging branches of giant trees formed a shady tunnel. We broke out into open farmland for a few miles and passed an enormous lake, and when we next entered the forest, it had a thicker, wilder look. The pavement gave way to a packed mud track at the Darién state line, flanked on both sides by an impenetrable wall of green.

Darién is the largest of Panama's provinces, but it is also among its poorest and least populated. Yaviza, with about fifteen hundred people, was Darién's second largest town. When residents wanted a taste of the big city, they could take a canoe down to La Palma, population forty-five hundred.

Despite its humble status, the province had a long and storied history. It was from a peak in Darién that Vasco Balboa in 1513 became the first European to spot the Pacific Ocean, and he later led an expedition through the jungle to reach those unexplored waters.

In 1698, Scotland tried to establish a colony in Darién in hopes of facilitating trade with Asia and pulling the country's financial bacon out of the fire after years of poor harvests. But most of the settlers died, the colony was abandoned, and the financial losses forced Scotland to hook its political wagon to England. More recently, the Darién jungle had become a refuge for Colombian rebels, which had riled up Panama's security forces.

Not long after we hit the mud, we came upon a clearing with a guard shack and a single soldier. The man marched out, checked our passports, and waved us on. There wasn't a whiff of corruption, no hint that money might need to change hands. He was completely professional, and he took my respect for the country up another notch.

The road got narrower and the jungle thicker. A long black snake flashed across our path, and when its head reached the trees its tail had barely left those on the other side. I pulled over at the spot where it disappeared and made what I thought was a fine suggestion, backed by a generous stipend, that Peter mosey on into the tall grass to see where the big fella went. He made his own suggestion, foul and disrespectful, yet somehow admirable in its profane complexity, especially considering that it was delivered in flawless Spanish. I was so proud.

After another hour the green walls opened up into another clearing. Two soldiers manned this checkpoint, and one walked briskly to my window and asked me where we were going. Told Yaviza, he frowned and asked to see inside our trunk. I hopped out and opened it, and he stared uncertainly at all the space, not only vacant but recently vacuumed. He waved his partner over and they checked beneath the seats. Finally, he pulled my knapsack off the back seat and laid it on the hood while the other man checked our passports.

I couldn't help but contrast the tight security at this lonely outpost with the loose affair in Las Tablas a few days earlier. About a hundred people had surrounded the president, Mireya Moscoso, as she spoke on a sidewalk in front of a public park. She was flanked by two bodyguards, but I saw none on the rooftops or in the park where hundreds of people partied in apparent ignorance of—or worse, from a security perspective, disdain for—their leader. Raucous groups of men were drinking beer, and an impressive collection of empties signaled they had been at it for a while. There weren't a lot of women in the park, though there were plenty of kids dodging around the adults in noisy games of tag.

When two ragged white beachcombers emerged from the bedlam and edged to within fifty feet of the president, the bodyguards paid them no more attention than anyone else. I could have walloped Moscoso with a grapefruit, which violated my minimum standard for presidential protection. If you can't stop a man with a citrus, you don't really have security.

But out here in Darién, the soldiers were on top of their game. As one rifled through my knapsack, the other fired off questions. Where were we from? When did we leave the United States? How long had we been in Panama?

Finally, he asked me what was really on his mind: Why I was taking my son into such a sketchy area? There had been kidnappings in the forest, and rebels had killed some people in a settlement a dozen miles from Yaviza.

"Why do you take a boy to such a place?" he asked with genuine concern.

Why indeed? Some might say we lacked reason enough even to justify exposure to the malaria that plagued the eastern jungles. Now we were adding the risk of violence. As the soldier spoke, I reconsidered our planned hike, but I still wanted to get to Yaviza. He knew the risks better than I did, however. If he insisted on turning us around, I wasn't going to make a stink, but first I was going to try to make him understand.

"My son and I have traveled thousands of miles on the road from the United States to this place here," I told him. "I just want to show him the end."

The hint of a smile touched the man's lips. He stared for a few seconds up the muddy strip we had driven in on and then down the muddy track toward Yaviza. His smile got bigger.

He chattered with his partner for a few moments before both turned and held out their hands.

"Good luck," they said and clapped us on the shoulder as we slid into the car.

The green walls again closed in, and we rolled deeper into Darién. Peter climbed into the backseat for a nap while I stared at the road ahead. I'd read that Latin American bandits liked to block a road with tree branches and attack drivers when they stopped, so I imagined hitting the brakes and slamming the car into reverse at the first glimpse of an obstruction. Except for a couple of trucks that splashed past going the other way, however, the road was empty.

I wondered about our reception in Yaviza. It was the childhood home of the dictator Manuel Antonio Noriega, who I'd been told had been good to the town during the years he ruled Panama. After the United States overthrew him in 1989 and hauled him to Miami for a short trial and a long prison sentence, Yaviza reverted to its natural state of neglected frontier hamlet. It seemed reasonable that the residents would hold a grudge.

I glanced at Peter, who was kicking his feet like a dreaming dog on the back seat, and worked out what I thought was a reasonable plan. We would drive into town to wherever the road ended, hop out, corral some passerby to take our picture, and jump back into the car. We would be back on the road in less than a minute, long before any bad guys knew we had even stopped by. With the windows rolled up, we'd be safe when the mosquitoes emerged at dusk.

We hit another checkpoint and then another, and the searches and questioning got more involved. Finally I was waved off the road into the shade of a concrete building and ordered out of the car. Soldiers checked our passports, searched our trunk, and ran through the usual list of questions. They seemed agitated, and when I told them we were headed for Yaviza they disappeared inside.

An officer came out a minute later and the interrogation resumed, but when I told him the full story he sighed, looked up the road, and went back inside. A minute later he reappeared and waved me in. I gestured to Peter to follow, but the officer shook his head, which seemed strange until he steered me into an office so tiny it was filled nearly wall to wall with a battered metal desk. He squeezed between the wall and the desk and slid into a wooden chair next to El Jefe, the highest-ranking National Police officer in the area. They gestured for me to take a seat across from them.

"The place you want to go is a little dangerous," El Jefe began in slow, deliberate Spanish. "There are guerrillas and kidnappers, and even if they are not there today, their cousins always are. It is not safe for Americans right now, especially a boy. An American boy would be very valuable to a kidnapper."

El Jefe was aching to turn us around, but by now I knew the magic words. I told him our story just as I had told the others, and just like the others he smiled. Maybe he had a son and had dreamed of taking a similar trip, or maybe he liked the idea of a young man finishing what he had started. Whatever the reason, El Jefe was on board. He nodded his head, had a hundred-and-fifty-mile-per-hour conversation with his lieutenant, and turned back to me.

"We have to ask you, sir. Do you have any weapons?"

Of course I didn't. With all the searches we had faced on Latin American roads, I would no more carry a weapon than a kilo of cocaine. So I told him no and looked for an approving nod. Instead, his eyes sprang wide and he threw his hands in the air. He shook his head in wonder as he chattered at his lieutenant, and I didn't need to understand the words to get the gist: this gringo is dumb as a coconut.

With a look of scorn, he reached down and yanked open a drawer. Out came an assortment of junk—broken ballpoint pens, a tangled ball of plastic-coated wire, the chipped black receiver from a phone—which he tossed atop his desk like the flotsam it was. When he laid down a battered pistol with a broken grip, he stared at me with eyebrows raised. I shook my head. I didn't know how to use the thing, and I didn't want to worry about it going off in my knapsack. Exasperated, he lowered his eyes and resumed his search for who knew what, and after a few more seconds swept the whole mess back into the drawer. Finally, he pulled a cell phone from his top pocket, laid it next to a pad on which he wrote his name and number, and slid both across the desk.

"When you get off the bus, look for the soldiers," he said. "Give them the phone and paper and tell them to call me." He stood up and shook my hand. "Good luck. You can leave your car where it is parked. I will watch it until you return."

"Leave my car?" I asked. "But I need to drive to Yaviza."

El Jefe and the lieutenant laughed. "You can drive away, but you will return on foot," El Jefe said. "The road beyond here is too muddy. It is not possible for cars. A bus will be here soon. Good luck."

● ● ●

"Thank you, Edmundo, for encouraging us to leave the Dart in Mexico," I said as we sat in the shade of a palm tree outside the police station. Peter shook his head with relief. We both knew that if we had blown all our money getting the car to Darién only to be stopped so close to the End of the Road, I'd have gunned it through the slop until we sank up to our doors.

"We need to send him a nice card," he said. "Or we could buy him a gift and drop it off on . . ."

His voice trailed off as a bus lurched toward us out of the trees at all of fifteen miles per hour, listing to the right and bouncing like Kmart's mechanical horse.

"Oh no," Peter whispered. "The Stench Bucket."

He grabbed his head with both hands and watched his nightmare trundle down the muddy road. It slid to a stop, and the ticket man kicked open the door, which appeared to have lost another screw from its bottom hinge.

"It's only fifteen miles, right?" Peter asked, eyes wide with panic. "Why don't we walk?"

But things weren't as bad as he feared. The San Miguelito crowd had gotten off somewhere along the way, leaving only the handful of people with whom we had left the Albrook terminal. No wonder the bus only ran once a week, and no wonder the driver picked up fares where he could along the way.

Everyone looked as though they were seeing ghosts when we climbed aboard.

"Where? . . . What?" the ticket man stammered as we hurried down the aisle to our former seats. The passengers stared at us as the bus trundled down the road. Even the driver was stealing wary glances in the mirror. All were dying to know the answer to the mystery, and all were wondering what tricks the crafty gringos might perform next. But the story seemed so convoluted and insulting as I ran it through my mind that I figured it was best left untold. Let them fill in the blanks, and they would conjure up a tale they could retell for years.

El Jefe wasn't kidding about the road. It became a bog within a mile, and we slipped and slid through mud that at times was two feet deep. When the wheels started spinning, the driver repeatedly slammed the gearshift between low and reverse and popped the clutch until the bus shook free. We stopped at one particularly swampy corner for fifteen min-utes to wait for a truck to pull another from the muck. When all was clear, the driver goosed it, and as we slipped through the turn the bus's back end nearly passed the front.

Finally, more than two hours after we had left the last checkpoint, we rounded a corner and rolled to a stop in a broad lot of packed dirt. To our right was the languid, brown Chucunaque River, its surface abuzz with flying insects. Directly in front was a collection of rickety tin structures that were perfectly cast for their role as the first buildings at the End of the Road. Twenty years of dreaming had led me to this spot, but I didn't cheer or dance or really even give the whole thing much thought. I was nervous, and now that we were here I just wanted to get out fast.

First we needed a photo, however. We got off the bus and set a course for the dock, but we hadn't gone far before three soldiers raced toward us from a walkway between the buildings. They spread out as they ran and skidded to a stop five feet away, two on one side and one on the other, and all three had slipped the rifles from their shoulders. What made them so skittish that they looked at two obvious tourists and saw Pablo Escobar and son? I never did figure that one out. I wanted to calmly nod at the jungle beyond the river and say, "Easy, guys, the trouble's out there."

I wanted to, but their anxiety was contagious. What I did was drop my knapsack and raise my hands, which I now know is on the short list of "worst things to do when confronted by twitchy soldiers."

The two on our flank raised their weapons as the third began barking orders I couldn't comprehend. I'm not sure what Peter was doing (yawn-ing, maybe?) because I didn't dare take my eyes off the guy in front. I pointed to the pack on the ground and shouted, "Teléphono!"

"I have a number for you to call," I stammered. "The commander wants to speak with you."

The leader squatted down and dumped the contents of my knapsack on the ground. He pulled the paper from between the jaws of the flip phone and stared at it quizzically before dialing the number.

The seconds passed like minutes as I watched the soldier hold the phone to his ear. Maybe El Jefe wasn't at his desk. Maybe his shift had ended and he'd gone home. In that case, my fishy behavior had probably earned us a long night in a cage.

But the soldier suddenly began chattering, and seconds later we were free to go. I thought ruefully that had El Jefe not spent fifteen minutes terrorizing me in his office I might not have lost my cool when the soldiers came, but the man had come through when it counted.

I asked an old fisherman to snap our photo on the dock, and then we hustled back to the bus. The driver had the hood up and was checking the oil, so we climbed aboard and walked back to our seats. A few minutes later the hood slammed down and the driver climbed onto the first step. He stood there in silence for a few seconds, glaring over the long line of seat backs.

"What are you doing?"

"Waiting to go back to Panama City. When do we leave?"

The man snorted, shook his head, and hit me with the same look I'd seen on El Jefe's face when I told him I was unarmed. "The bus leaves in three days," he said. "Now get off. You can't sleep here."

We wandered up Yaviza's main drag past a rogue's gallery of solemn faces behind the dusty screens of rickety shacks. We surprised a group of men playing dice in the doorway of a general store, and their wolfish looks of interest convinced me that walking deeper into the settlement was a bad idea. We turned around and walked back toward the dock, next to which sat a restaurant built beneath a giant *palapa*. We ducked under the thatched roof, and I asked a few patrons if they knew of anyone driving out of town that night. They just stared, so we turned around and headed back outside.

"Wait," said a voice from the back. A pretty black teenager came out of the kitchen, wiping her hands on an apron. "Go to where the road comes out of the trees. Someone might leave and you can ask for a ride."

I thanked her and turned to go, but she stopped us again.

"Where are you from?" she asked in slow, clear Spanish. I told her, and she asked more questions about America and what we had seen on the way down. As I gave my tortured, hesitant answers, her eyes would drift from mine to something behind me. They returned to me only when I stopped talking. She then would ask another question, and her eyes would slide off my shoulder until I was done rambling. I figured it was a cultural thing—women in Darién don't look men in the eye—but I couldn't have been more off the mark. When I finished what turned out to be my final answer she spoke again, but this time she didn't look at me.

"Your son is very handsome," she cooed, and I felt a surge of pity for the poor girl. Stuck out here in the jungle, a vitamin A deficiency had obviously left her with the eyes of . . .

"Handsome like his papa."

. . . an eagle! There must be something in the water that made her vision so keen and her mind so sharp!

"If you don't get a ride, then come back here," the girl said as she watched Peter examine his shuffling feet. "My mother will rent you a room in my house."

I thanked her for her kind offer, shook her warm hand, and stared hard at Peter as we walked the hundred or so yards to the edge of the trees. How that kid had changed in three months! Six-foot-one and muscular, his square jaw anchored a symmetrical face whose acne had vanished nearly as quickly as it had arrived. His deep tan was an appealing contrast to his perfect white teeth. His broad shoulders rode high and square yet loose and natural, no longer forced like a new Marine's. He carried himself with a quiet confidence that said without boast or challenge that after what he'd been through, he was ready for anything.

Without either of us really noticing, the boy had grown up.

"What?" he asked with a perplexed smile when he noticed my glistening eyes. I was struck by a need to say something profound, inspiring words on his coming of age that would live forever in Millson family lore.

It was a fleeting urge that I smothered in its crib.

"You have a weird bug on your shoulder," I said as I brushed past, leaving him tugging uncertainly at his shirt while I hurried ahead to snag the best seat on a flat rock by the road.

Are there families outside of sappy TV dramas where dads manage to deliver emotional declarations to sons without one or the other squirming with embarrassment? Not in my world. The best I could manage was to tell Peter I was proud of him once in a while, though by always doing it in Spanish it might not have packed the same punch. Our months together had done wonders for our relationship, but we would never be Ward and Beaver Cleaver.

We sat by the road and watched the sun sink closer to the treetops, and I tried not to think about the jungle full of anopheles mosquitoes that would soon wake up hungry for blood. We had been taking an antimalarial drug called chloroquine since leaving the Guatemalan highlands, but the malaria in Darién was immune. Mefloquine was the drug of choice here, but taking chloroquine and mefloquine together could cause hallucinations.

Had I thought we might be stranded in the open at dusk, I would have risked a little temporary derangement, but I had originally planned to be safely behind the screens of a park service hut by then, so I hadn't bought any mefloquine.

I glanced again at the setting sun and figured we had another twenty minutes. No sense panicking yet. We had plenty of time for another geographical wager, and this time I was prepared. A cantina in Panama City had decorated part of a wall with a world map, which I'd studied carefully for the fifteen seconds it took for the exasperated bartender to change a rum-soaked fifty-dollar bill.

"For five bucks," I began grandly, and Peter's eyes narrowed with interest, "correctly answer the following questions. If you get even one correct, you win the money, but if you bomb all three you owe me five. Ready?"

"Wait!" he said, then proposed a convoluted series of amendments whose end result—higher stakes if he won, lower if he didn't—I only managed to unravel long after I lost the bet. (For the record, Yaviza lies east of Miami; south of Caracas, Venezuela; and less than a quarter of a degree north of the beach in Costa Rica's Corcovado National Park). We were arguing over the payoff when a dump truck trundled across the flats from the river. We jumped up and waved, and the truck's brakes shrieked as it rolled to a stop.

The truck had no tailgate, which made it easy to scramble into the bed. We picked our way around some hunks of scrap metal to the front and called to the driver, who advised us to hang on before easing the truck into a shuddering start. And hang we did. Arched across the top of the bed were two pipes to which the driver could lash a tarp, and we dangled from one to keep our feet clear of the bouncing avalanche of toe-squashing junk.

El Jefe and a few other soldiers were lounging outside in the light of an open doorway when we pulled up two hours later, and all broke into a rousing cheer when they saw Peter climb out of the truck. With all the backslapping and handshaking, we felt like astronauts just home from the moon. El Jefe had filled the others in, and we spent twenty minutes answering questions about all the countries we had seen.

"So now you go home," El Jefe said, and I almost replied, "No, we still have another month," but it suddenly hit me that he was right. From this point on, we would be working our way north and west instead of south and east, and the destination was not some mysterious place on a map but the same unsettled life I had fled.

We had made it to the End of the Road, but I was in no mood for celebrating. All I could think of was that I was on my way back to the other end. The dead end.

SEVENTEEN

The barmaid's eyes didn't so much as flick my way when I ordered, and when she returned, she set my beer in front of Peter. She stared as he drained half the bottle in two swigs, and her chest heaved as he set it down with a big smile. I could almost see the heat radiating from her supple young body as she took her ripe lower lip between her teeth, but when her dreamboat belched loudly in my ear, the spell was broken.

"How old is he?" she whispered as her head whipped around in panic. It was a question I would hear a lot in the next few weeks. Told thirteen, she groaned and dumped the rest of the beer in a plastic cup for me. Still flustered, she set the empty bottle back in front of Peter.

I shot a few perplexed glances his way as I finished my beer. He was a fine-looking kid, all right, but that didn't begin to explain the reactions of the girl in Yaviza, the desperate mother on the road, or this smitten waitress five years his senior.

"C'mon," I said. I slid off my stool and ducked under the lip of the beach bar's *palapa*. I was eager to resume an important discussion we'd been having, and distracted females were too distracting. We wandered up a hill toward the second oldest church in the Western Hemisphere, which was the reason we had come to Panama's island of Taboga, but I wasn't thinking about history. The only thing on my mind since we'd made the turn in Yaviza was what I was going to do when I got home.

"Have you thought of anything?" I asked as we peered through the door of the humble, whitewashed landmark.

"I have," Peter said, and he cleared his throat theatrically. "Open a Hobo Emporium. You're an expert on the style, and you already have the inventory!"

I left him doubled over in giggles and walked inside to take a seat on one of the polished wooden pews.

"Please, Lord," I whispered. "Give me the patience not to strangle my son."

In fairness to Peter, my anxiety was getting old, and up until now he'd taken the question seriously. He'd even offered a couple of memorable suggestions, which made up in imagination for what they lacked in practicality. There was "Rent-a-Raptor," which would provide harried neighbors with a permanent solution to the yapping of little dogs. All we would need was an endangered harpy eagle and some quality training time. Then there was "Suckers," a restaurant with nothing on the menu but deep-fried squid and octopus. If anyone complained about paying twenty bucks for a bowl full of slippery tentacles, Peter would run out and shout, "Suckers!"

Peter joined me in the pew, and we stared for a while at what by Latin American church standards was a lackluster interior. At the front was a colorful display of statues, but the view was marred by several square wood pillars that held up an industrial metal roof. Renovations had stripped it of any charm it might have had in the early 1500s, but it was out of the sun, so we settled in.

A half-dozen high school girls were a few rows ahead, probably there on a field trip. They sat as sedately as nuns until one happened to glance around and spot the young gringo, abruptly morphing them into a whispering cluster of swiveling heads.

Peter developed an abrupt urge for more sightseeing, so we walked back out to stare at the whitewashed houses on the hillside above the beach. The place lacked the dramatic ruins of Old Panama, but its history was just as colorful. Francisco de Almagro left from Taboga in 1526 to conquer the Incas. Both Henry Morgan and Sir Francis Drake used it as a base before pillaging Panama City, and the French impressionist Paul Gauguin once called it home.

At the top of one narrow lane, I glanced back and saw Peter's fans from the church coming up the hill behind us. When we turned a corner they must have sprinted, because when they reappeared they were a lot closer. They stopped when we stopped and moved when we moved until finally someone lost a coin flip. An emissary emerged from the laughing pack, slapping at the hands propelling her. She smoothed her white shirt, straightened her plaid skirt, took one last deep breath, and shuffled ahead.

She walked toward me, but her eyes never left Peter, and her words poured out in a rush with the breath she had been holding.

"You are not from here?" she asked, and I smiled and shook my head. Contact made, the rest of the girls surged forward. Peter turned quickly away, having suddenly discovered a fascinating insect on a nearby bougainvillea, but the girls were undeterred. One after another, they followed up with rapid-fire questions:

"What's his name?"

"How old is he?"

"Where is he from?"

"What is he doing here?"

To which I replied:

"Pedro."

"Seventeen."

"Hollywood."

"Looking for a girlfriend."

The girls squealed and enveloped Peter like meat bees on a hunk of tuna. They mashed him in a group hug, ran their hands through his hair, and kissed his cheeks. Appalled but unable to work himself loose, he stood there like a dog getting a bath until they'd had their fill and moved on.

"I know what I'm going to do when I get home," I said as I watched the girls giggle their way back to the church. Peter was rubbing his cheeks with the backs of his palms and looking thoroughly disgusted.

"What?"

"Open a boy-dello! I already have the inventory!"

I cackled madly and grabbed my sides and slapped my knee, but Peter didn't see the humor. He muttered something under his breath and walked down to the dock to join the line for the next ferry.

What was going on with the girls of Panama? I had no idea, but I sure was enjoying the show. Peter's sudden sex appeal was undeniable, but it remained a mystery until years later when I stumbled across an article in *The Economist* magazine that offered a plausible theory. "Why Women in Dirty Places Like Brad Pitt" detailed a study claiming that females in the developing world get all shook up over masculine men. Broad shoulders, strong jaws, height, and muscle promise protection and robust children, and Peter topped that off with uncommon self-assurance and a boy-band smile.

I believe the final magic ingredient was added on our drive to Yaviza when Peter realized he was turning the corner on his long ordeal and heading home for Christmas. An infusion of pure joy put a spit shine on his new looks and confidence, and suddenly I was traveling with Elvis.

There never was a more reluctant rock star, however. After Taboga he vetoed further excursions and holed up in our hotel room in Panama City. He was adamant that something was wrong with Panamanian women and that things would calm down once we left the country. And to his great relief, he was right. We spent a few long and uneventful days hopping from bus to cheap hotel to bus on our way north, and he suffered no indignities greater than some batted eyelashes from desk clerks and fellow riders. By the time we got to Santa Rosa, Honduras, his Panama problems were forgotten.

Founded in the early 1700s by tobacco growers, the pretty colonial town was built on hills in the western highlands. Terra-cotta roofs rolled like pink waves into the distance from the town's high ground, and the cobblestoned streets came together at a cozy central park. We lounged on a bench in the shade of an interesting mix of hardwoods and palms while I daydreamed aloud about living in such a peaceful place.

"We ought to look around for some land where I can grow tobacco," I mused as I stretched my arms across the bench back.

"You can't even keep Mom's houseplants alive when she's away," Peter grumbled. He wasn't about to let me so much as think about moving to a country where he couldn't ski.

"Yeah, you're probably right," I said. I eased my right foot off my left ankle, paused so as not to overexert myself, and slid my left foot atop my right. I yawned. What a relaxing little town.

"I probably ought to stick with livestock. I'll bet this is good cattle country."

Peter had heard enough. "C'mon. Get up," he said, shoving me half off the bench before leaping to his feet. "Let's go find an Internet café. I want to check the snow totals in Utah."

He made me lead the way so I wouldn't get distracted and wander into the feed store. But the Internet wasn't working, so we turned around and walked back to a boot shop near the park. The sole on one of Peter's ninety-dollar sneakers was coming loose, a fact made more annoying when we saw the price of a handmade pair of full-leather, guaranteed-for-life cowboy boots: Just sixty dollars.

"Maybe I could be that guy's apprentice and learn to make boots," I said as we walked out of the shop with Peter's shoe as good as new. The repair had taken five minutes and cost fifty cents. "You could be the delivery boy, and Mom and Hannah . . ."

"I'll buy you dinner if you promise to shut up," Peter snapped, and I had to chuckle.

"Well, now. It looks like the shoe's on the other—ow!"

I was still rubbing the new welt on my shoulder as we entered a tiny restaurant a few blocks from the park. It was early, and the place was empty. The family that ran it was in the back getting ready for the dinner crowd, so I stood near the cash register while Peter ducked into the bathroom. When the thirty-something proprietress came out from the kitchen, she shook my hand and led me to a seat at one of the room's four tables. She asked where I was from and what had brought me to Santa Rosa, which led to a minute of pleasant chitchat that abruptly ended when her eyes grew wide and her train of thought fell off the trestle. I didn't have to turn around to know the cause. I'd seen that look enough to know that Elvis had just stepped into the room and that my odds of getting the beer I'd ordered had just dropped.

"This is your son," she said, though she wasn't really talking to me anymore. She watched him slide into his chair as she backed into the kitchen, and a moment later a teenage waitress came stumbling out, arms flailing, after an enthusiastic shove from behind.

The girl regained her balance and hissed something over her shoulder before turning and catching sight of the golden-haired gringo at the table. Then she froze, but only for an instant, before smoothing her apron and moving forward with as much dignity as she could muster.

The waitress was about eighteen and a dead ringer for her fetching mother. She asked me a few questions and nodded politely at my answers, but I could tell from her darting eyes that she didn't hear a word. Two other females—one a little older, the other about twelve—came out of the kitchen and made a show of rearranging the silverware on a nearby table before everyone disappeared into the back.

"I'm thinking that if you at least smiled at your fans we might get a few extra tortillas," I whispered, but Peter wasn't amused. His ears reddened, and he stared at the sugar bag he'd been folding and unfolding for the past minute.

I chuckled quietly until the waitress returned with a glass of soda instead of my beer and a hunk of pork instead of my chicken tamale. I noticed that Peter's order was perfect, however, and when the girl served it she bent low and tipped her head in a fruitless attempt to catch his eye.

"Do you want something else to drink?" she asked hopefully.

"No, thank you," Peter whispered without raising his head.

She stood there uncertainly for a moment before disappearing into the kitchen. The mother was back in an instant, and she got straight to the point.

"How old is your son?" she asked as she looked him up and down like a hog buyer at a farm auction.

A movement behind the woman caught my eye. The door to the kitchen was barely ajar, and I imagined three sets of dark eyes watching us through the crack.

I turned back to the mother. "Thirteen."

Her eyes widened, and she repeated the number softly before turning and shouting it at the door. Shrieks and laughter erupted from the kitchen, and the teen stumbled out red-faced but smiling a few moments later.

From that day on, in the interest of efficiency and accurate orders, I greeted every moon-eyed waitress with, "The boy is thirteen."

♥ ♥ ♥

The days ran together as we made our way north. No one accosted Peter on our bus rides, and by the time we got to Tapachula, Mexico, it seemed that his woman troubles were finally over. My only concern by then was that the car was where we'd left it and that we could make it through the country without getting robbed.

"We've already been robbed," Peter proclaimed as we lugged our packs away from the bus station. "No way that car is still there."

But it was, though we had a hard time spotting it at first. The old man's yard had staged a renaissance in the past six weeks, and waist-high weeds rose unbroken from the street to his front porch. Except for the Dart's windows and roof, barely visible above the weed tops, it looked like the photo of prime *fer-de-lance* habitat I'd admired in a Costa Rican snake exhibit.

Peter had seen the same photo, so I didn't bother asking him to wade over to the shack. But just about the time I had screwed up the courage to do it myself, I noticed the old man dozing in the shade of his porch.

"Hello!" I called. "We have returned for the car."

The old man's head rose up, and in an instant he was coming through the weeds like monster bait in a horror movie. I cringed, expecting his torso to snap back and disappear at any moment, but he made it to the edge in one piece.

He shook our hands and waved at the yard in embarrassment, apologizing for the weeds but insisting that we were a year early. He trotted back to his shack and reemerged with a machete, with which he dispatched the snake refuge around the Dart in a matter of minutes. But even after I paid him the twenty dollars I owed, he didn't rest. He grabbed a rag from the porch and cleaned the dust from our windows, headlights, and taillights. When he was done, he shook our hands again and made us promise to come back for a visit.

The old man was the perfect ambassador for our return to a country I had written off six weeks earlier as a hostile den of swindlers. He couldn't have been nicer, and neither could anyone else we met that day. When I overpaid for drinks at a store, the owner followed me onto the sidewalk to give me my change. A security guard at an insurance company chased us three blocks in the demonic heat to bring us back to the office, where we discovered that the amiable agent who had reluctantly sent us away had figured out how to write a policy for a single week.

Peter was happier than I was to be back in Mexico, where he had a five-week track record of no trouble with females. He calmly strolled up the Tapachula sidewalk secure in his invisibility, but he was really just oblivious.

The females of Tapachula weren't as forward as their cousins to the south, but they were every bit as interested. They stopped and stared and elbowed their less observant friends, and heads popped out from every other doorway Peter passed. But he didn't offer anyone the least bit of encouragement, so I began taking note of loose roof tiles and rickety structures to avoid. God could not be pleased that the little ingrate was squandering his gift. I expected an earthquake.

And sure enough, while walking back to our hotel from the insurance agency, my knees began to quiver.

Leaning on the doorframe of a beauty parlor, studying her perfect nails, was the most gorgeous woman I'd ever seen outside of movies and magazines. She was about eighteen with long dark hair, big brown eyes, and plump red lips, and she looked bored beyond tears with life in this broiling border town.

I was in the lead, but she never saw me. Her eyes swept past my shoulder, and she gasped as though she'd been doused with ice water.

When it came to man-bait, that gal had been blessed with a full tackle box, and she dangled every lure in the path of the tall, blonde stranger who was coming her way. She set her mouth in a shy half smile and batted her long eyelashes. Her lithe torso snapped to attention, and a subtle half-turn left one shapely thigh and two perky breasts jutting into the walkway.

I was legless. For the first time in my forty-three years, I knew exactly what I wanted to be when I grew up: Peter. But he slipped past me without a word and continued up the sidewalk without a glance at the goddess in the doorway. Her face fell as she swung around to watch him amble away, and she took two hesitant steps before stopping herself and slumping against the building, spirit crushed like a bug.

It was a gut-wrenching sight, and if I could have figured out a way to skin that boy without causing too much commotion, I'd have sewn me a Peter suit and gone back to console the pretty little thing. I imagine she wound up marrying a taco vendor instead of the drug lord who was in her future before Peter's indifference destroyed her confidence.

♥ ♥ ♥

Even today I feel guilty about badmouthing the mighty Dart. Sure, it was a gas-guzzler, but that's only because it was built when fuel cost fifteen cents a gallon. Thirty years later it still had the oomph to carry us more than three thousand miles to Guatemala, and its only mechanical problem was an alternator that I had allowed to get wet. After sitting for six weeks in tropical weeds, it roared to life with the first turn of the key. That car was one of the most dependable vehicles ever built.

Climbing into the front seat the next morning made us a little giddy. We were sick of riding buses, and Peter was happy with the anonymity provided by his own transportation. He rapped on the dash to the beat of some Mexican hillbilly music as we rolled up the long, lonely isthmus highway, and at some point I began stomping my foot.

I was about to belt out some lyrics to accompany the music when a hundred million ants swarmed onto the seat. They had moved into the car during its weeks in the weeds, and they didn't appreciate the stomping. In fact, I'd have to say they found it irritating, because a few hundred remained on the floor to maul our sandaled feet.

The attack provoked some erratic steering, which caught the attention of the soldiers at an army checkpoint, and a few seconds later I was trying to convince the commander that he had not just captured a drunken driver. The misunderstanding was resolved when a private sent to search the Dart screamed like a tweenie at a Justin Bieber concert, though that led to even more confusion.

"Why are you transporting ants?" demanded the commander as he peered through the open passenger door. "Do you have a permit?"

The vanguard of the horde had scaled the front seat and led the way down the back, and apparently it had caught up to the stragglers under the seat because the flow of the creepy brown river never ebbed. Another group ran up a doorframe, crossed the ceiling, and sprinted down the other side before rejoining the main body somewhere on the floor.

My explanation led to a lot more questions and a demand to see our passports, which the man studied for so long that I got impatient. What was the point of this charade? We both knew that this play would end with me forking over twenty bucks, so why not just save some time and drop the freakin' curtain?

"What's the problem?" I demanded.

The commander looked up with a friendly smile, the last expression I expected.

"You have been all the way to Panama and back," he said as he handed me the passports. "I have always wanted to see that road."

"We went to the end, almost to Colombia," I said, and his smile broadened. I spent the next fifteen minutes answering questions about all the countries we had seen until he got around to the grand finale: "So which is your favorite?"

There was only one right answer in that situation—"Mexico! The people are the best!"—so I didn't hesitate. Besides, it wasn't as big a stretch as it would have been the last time we passed through.

The commander shook my hand and yelled something to the private, who ran into the guard shack and reappeared with a metal cask in one hand and a rubber hose in the other. He filled the Dart with a cloud of third-world pesticide, and they sent us on our way without asking for a dime. Mexico was growing on me.

♥ ♥ ♥

The drive from Tapachula to Juchitán was long and hot but relaxing compared with the reverse trip two and a half months before. Peter talked nonstop about ski gear when he wasn't napping, and I just nodded and threw in an occasional "Uh-huh," "hmm," or "okay" while enjoying the weird mix of desert and jungle scenery that I'd probably never see again.

When we stopped for the night in the same hotel we'd stayed at on the way down, we shared an unsettling feeling that the past few months had been a dream. Except for the desk clerk hitting on Peter, everything was the same as before. When she put us in our old room, we went right for the closet to look at all the useless items we had off-loaded from the Dart. It was almost shocking to find nothing there.

Peter got excited as we got closer to Oaxaca because he had a lot of pent-up shopper's anxiety. He hadn't spent much in the past few months because he would have had to carry anything he bought, but now his long-awaited spree was near. He could fill up the back seat with souvenirs for all I cared. The only border crossing left was America's.

Oaxaca's dry season had arrived while we were gone, and the hills were as brown as Utah's in August. We got a hotel on the outskirts and rode a bus to the city center, where the sellers of purple wooden toads and orange dragons were about to have a big afternoon. When we got off and wandered into the central park, I was walloped by a wave of déjà vu. A few men were arguing with the shoeshine guy in the Cruz Azul soccer jersey. Artisans lined the main drag with their wares spread across folding tables or blankets on the ground, and a clutch of high school girls in white shirts and plaid skirts swayed to the music of a longhaired youth strumming his guitar. It was the identical scene from our first day in town three and a half months before—and it lasted for about fifteen seconds.

The musician's back was to us, which gave me a perfect view of the moment the girls went deaf. They glided around both sides of the bewildered youth, reformed behind him like wolves on the hunt, and stopped a few paces in front of us.

If I'd needed any more evidence of Peter's dramatic transformation, this was it. The few Oaxaca females who had even noticed him three months before had curled their lips with disdain. Now they were smiling shyly and batting their eyes, and it was Peter's lip that was curling.

"You are not from here?" one began, and after the usual formalities, she asked if she could take the young phenom's picture.

"Why not?" I said, ignoring the daggers in Peter's eyes. I herded the reluctant celebrity toward a spot of shade beneath a tree and stepped back to watch him fidget. The photographer was lining up the shot when another girl sneaked into the frame and put her arm around Peter's waist. Before the camera girl could adjust the frame, two friends came running in from the other side, then four more, then another three. The kid's exasperated head was the only part of him visible in that writhing mass of hormones, and the photographer looked just as put out. Finally she tossed me the camera and leapt into the mob.

"Let's get out of here," Peter said after the girls let him go, and he started speed walking toward the central market. He picked up a couple of new admirers in the first block, but he was going so fast it took them four more to catch up.

"Why don't you slow down?" I suggested as I glanced over my shoulder at the laboring pair. "You're going to ruin those poor girls' makeup."

But Peter wasn't listening. He was staring straight ahead with deep concern, and his lips had curled into a "Are you freakin' kiddin' me?" grimace.

A tour bus was in the intersection about thirty yards ahead, waiting to make a left turn. It was rocking like a paint mixer, and hysterical teens were mashed against the big front window, pounding on the glass. Every side window was filled with the head and arm of one frenzied female and half the head of another trying to force her way out. The air vibrated with the screams of girls gone wild.

I stood listening to the commotion recede as the bus rolled away. I wish I could say I had the presence of mind to come up with an appropriate wisecrack, but I was speechless. Even though I'd been front and center for the Farewell Tour of the Heartbreak Kid for two weeks now, I couldn't accept what I had just seen.

One of the stalkers tugged on my sleeve. She politely asked a few questions before handing me a camera and making a squirming Peter sandwich with her friend. I wanted to tell him to enjoy the attention, that someday he would trade a kidney for a tenth of this incredible power, but his expression told me not to bother. He could not have looked more uncomfortable if he were getting a public colonoscopy.

"How about some lunch?" I suggested as we watched the young women hurry away. Peter just nodded, so I nudged him toward the door to the market. We wandered past the rug sellers and mescal stalls to the area where they peddled vegetables, meat, and live chickens. We bought two plates of tacos and headed for the park.

We strolled past the market's weathered brick facade and rounded the corner. Fifty feet ahead, a hundred young maidens were bunched next to the tour bus. One looked our way and screamed, and an instant later the whole mob was shrieking down the sidewalk like a Catholic schoolgirls' reenactment of the battle scene from *Braveheart*.

"What the . . . ?" I began as I turned toward Peter, but a plate of tacos was spinning in the air where he'd just been. I caught a glimpse of him rounding the corner as his lunch splattered on the sidewalk, and then my own plate was knocked from my hands by a roiling torrent of delirious young women.

When I finally found him hiding behind a rug stand in the market, he'd had enough. We hurriedly bought a few Christmas gifts, caught a cab back to our hotel, loaded up the Dart, and sped out of town. Peter hadn't even paused to buy souvenirs for himself.

❤ ❤ ❤

For the next two days, Peter refused to leave the car unless it was to duck into the weeds to pee or to dash into our hotel room for the night. He lived on bread and cheese and whatever was cooking at roadside stands, but we had to cut that out after he ate some bad tamales. Within an hour, he was throwing up, and I had to stop early in Tuxpan so he could ride it out in bed.

I left him in the room and went out to buy something to settle his stomach. I had seen a pharmacy when we drove in, but I couldn't remember where it was. A cab driver was leaning against his car in front of the hotel reading a newspaper, but I hated to go that route. Whatever the guy charged me would be too much, and I'd spend the rest of the night grumbling about getting cheated. I walked right past.

"Where are you going, friend?"

I stopped and took a cleansing breath before turning around.

"The pharmacy."

"I will take you there for fifty pesos. It is a long walk, and the streets are not safe."

I had to smile. Compared with where we'd been, Tuxpan's streets were about as scary as a day care. And while I wasn't sure where the pharmacy was, I knew it wasn't a five-dollar ride away.

"Ten pesos," I said. "I don't want to buy your cab. I just want a ride."

The cabbie was a cool customer. He just shook his head and went back to his paper. I stood there uncertainly for a second before I regained my composure and turned to go. In Panama City one night I had stormed off into one of the worst slums in the hemisphere after a driver insisted on two fifty for a two-dollar ride, so this guy didn't have a prayer. I'd walk all afternoon through this peaceful town before I paid fifty pesos.

"Twenty-five," he said, and I hesitated. It was still too high, but I liked the direction of the negotiations.

I shook my head and resumed my walk, but I knew the hook had been set. When he called "fifteen," my mind shrieked in victorious exultation. Finally, after twenty years of travels, I had gotten the best of a Mexican cabbie. I was so pleased with myself that my head barely fit through the door as I climbed into the car. I paid the fifteen pesos and settled against the seat to revel in my victory.

It was a short celebration. The guy drove half a block, rounded the corner, and pulled to the curb in front of the pharmacy, having traveled not more than eighty feet. The second I stepped out he backed around the corner to his former spot.

I glanced up and down the street and was grateful to see that there had been no witnesses. I bought some pills in the pharmacy and started to walk back to the hotel, but a light down the block caught my eye. It was a cantina, and a cold beer might wash away the bitter taste from my cab ride. Besides, the cabbie might go away if I delayed my ignominious return for a few minutes. I strolled down the street and pushed through the door.

It was a long, narrow place, and every table between me and the bar in the back was packed with men. I felt the weight of a hundred eyes as I slalomed through the tables, and I was grateful for the *narcocorrido* blaring from the jukebox because it masked the unsettling fact that everyone had stopped talking. I knew now that this was a bad idea, but I couldn't just turn and run for the door. I decided to keep my cool, guzzle one beer, and then stroll back out like I owned the place.

The barmaid was a short, plump woman with buckteeth and a lazy eye, and I didn't like the crazy glint in the one that was pointing at me. She came around the bar, guided me to a nearby table with a hand on my butt, and elbowed some poor guy out of his chair. The man, who was very drunk, did not seem the least bit surprised, much less offended. When he regained his balance he tottered back over and draped an arm across my shoulders.

"Amigo," he slurred. "Take me with you to America."

His friend, a weird little dude with no front teeth, aimed a bizarre grin at me from across the table before suddenly rising up and attempting a Michael Jackson moonwalk.

Where was the waitress with that beer? I leaned back in my chair and squinted in a vain attempt to penetrate the darkness of the doorway behind the bar. There was nothing threatening about the scene—not yet, anyway—but such strong interest in one wayward gringo seemed an unhealthy harbinger.

"Amigo," the drunk said, giving my shoulders a little shake. "Amigo."

"Sorry, friend, I don't have a car," I lied. "Maybe you would like to walk with me to Texas."

The drunk's eyes fixed me with a disappointed stare before losing traction and sliding off to the side. He staggered in the direction of the bar and was nearly trampled as the barmaid galloped from the back room. She had freshened up her makeup—with an assist from Barnum & Bailey from the looks of it—and was patting her stringy hair while undoing the top buttons on her blouse.

Someone tapped her arm as she hurried past, and she sneered. Another guy yelled for a refill, and she stripped off her apron with one meaty hand and threw it at him. She set my beer on the table, crawled onto my lap, and began rubbing my chest. When she wasn't murmuring lewd suggestions, she was bellowing insults at the other patrons, and all I could do was struggle to make sense of it all.

And then it hit me. I must have been doused with some of the babe magnet's mojo, but in reacting with my middle-aged hide the formula had gone horribly wrong.

I was a hag magnet!

I shot out of my chair and spilled her onto the floor. No longer concerned with gracious exits, I raced like a thief for the door, pursued by the raucous laughter of fifty drunks and the furious insults of the jilted barmaid. I'd seen my last cantina on this trip.

♥ ♥ ♥

Peter had recovered by morning, so we got back on the road. We left the tropical forest not far north of Tuxpan and drove for hours through terrain that looked like Iowa.

In a restaurant south of Tampico, two men spent ten minutes describing a route north to Victoria that would not only spare us a huge toll but save us an hour of driving as well. Halfway through, another man wandered over to clarify a point. When we drove off, all three stood in the gravel and waved us on our way.

The kindness of the Mexicans on our return journey had spurred a lot of self-reflection. Had I just been so stressed out and protective of Peter on the way down that I had brought out the worst in everyone? I wasn't sure, but there was no doubt that the return trip had a different feel. Instead of bickering with crooked cops and colliding with macho men on sidewalks, I was laughing with schoolgirl stalkers and enjoying every second with my old/new BFF.

The only thing that could have made me happier would have been a road map for the rest of my life. But we'd pretty much exhausted all the career ideas, so it was looking like I'd be going back to the night shift. Unless . . .

"Hey, what do you think about me being a tour guide?" I asked Peter, which caused him to pass a gulp of water through his nose.

"Let's see," he began after he stopped coughing. "We stayed in dives and lived on dog food; you almost got us eaten by wild pigs; I was mugged; we were chased through the streets by a bandit; we were robbed by crooked cops, threatened by soldiers, and flimflammed at the border; you got us in a car crash; you ruined half our money in that oil can; and you booked a stench bucket to take us to a jungle full of Colombian rebels."

"Yeah, that was a great trip," I agreed, and he snorted.

"Just make sure you get paid in advance if you take somebody else."

We crossed the Tropic of Cancer just south of Ciudad Victoria, and the air took on a crispness we hadn't felt in months. The traffic built as we drove toward the border town of Matamoros, and before we knew it we were across the Rio Grande and rolling up to the US customs station.

The agent took one look at the Dart and waved us to a nearby lot, where we waited a few minutes for him to round up a drug-sniffing dog. The delay made me nervous, and I thought about how easy it would have been for someone to hide a few kilos of cocaine in the Dart's doorframes in Tapachula and then ambush us in the Texas desert if we made through customs.

There's nothing like a paranoid fantasy to give your eyes the shifty quality that feds find so irresistible. The agent was soon joined by two others, and even when the dog struck out, they couldn't let go of the notion that I must be guilty of something. One disappeared into the main building with our passports to do a little computer research while two others took us aside for separate interrogations.

As the agent led Peter a few feet away, I witnessed a transformation as stark as Cinderella's when the clock struck midnight. The unflappable young man became a nervous kid again. His feet shuffled and his eyes gleamed, and for a few seconds he couldn't answer a question. It was as if now, safely back on US soil, he could finally let down his guard.

He composed himself quickly, but something had changed. He was still square-shouldered and handsome, but unmistakably a boy. He caught the eye of some girls in a Brownsville restaurant, but after a few giggles they went back to their gossip. Peter could not have been more relieved.

We both were in a hurry to get home now that we were back in the states, but we were still a long way off. It took two days just to cross Texas, and a snowstorm near El Paso derailed my plans to save a few bucks by camping out. We stayed a night in New Mexico and another with a friend in Phoenix, and then a blizzard forced us to hole up in southern Utah. Finally, at noon on December 23, we drove up our snowy street and pulled into our driveway exactly four months and four hours after we had left.

I was a little slower out of the car than Peter, so I stood in the driveway and watched him bound up the steps to hug his mom and sister. He was a different person than the kid who had left in August, and though the trip had not affected me as profoundly, it had opened my eyes. I might be cursed to pine forever for some vague ideal of life, but I now could see that I already had the hard part licked. My job wasn't perfect and probably never would be, but my family sure was. And for the first time in years, I could honestly say that I was a pretty good father.

EPILOGUE

H ey, Dad."

"Hey, buddy," I whispered into the receiver so as not to disturb my fellow copyeditors. "How was school?"

"Okay. I got a hundred on the algebra test. When do you get off tonight?"

"A hundred? Way to kick its butt! I think that makes four in a row, right?"

"Uh-huh. When are you coming home?"

For months after the trip, the first thing Peter did when he walked into the house each afternoon was call me at work. I don't remember much about the conversations, only that I could set my watch by those 3:15 p.m. calls and that they were the highlight of my day. For Alison, watching that long-dormant ember flare up and burn stronger than ever was worth all her sacrifices while we were away.

Summer came, and the calls became sporadic. Sometime after Peter entered high school that fall, they stopped altogether. Like a lot of teenagers, including his sister when she reached high school, he wanted nothing to do with someone he suddenly realized might just be the biggest dork on the planet.

But here's the good part: from the day we got back from Central America, I never spent a minute worrying about Peter's future. He returned to school in January 2003 so far ahead of his class that it hadn't caught up by June. He was an A student from then on and earned a merit scholarship to the University of Utah, where he graduated with degrees in biomedical engineering and chemistry. What's next? Graduate school, medical school—or a sweet gig with a medical devices company? He's not sure, but after years of hard work, he has paved himself a golden path to the future.

That the path began with thousands of miles of bad asphalt and a muddy track through the jungle sounds implausible even to me. Getting mugged and menaced by robbers, drunks, and crooked cops while living in third-world hovels is obviously not an ideal situation for a boy's development.

So why did it work for Peter? Readers already know my charming personality had nothing to do with it, so I won't even try to go there. Ditto for my boundless wisdom. This book documents four months of screwing up every day, 24/7.

But those last few words—more than the tens of thousands that came before—are the key: I was with Peter every day, 24/7—completely immersed in his life. Weighed against that fact, my screwups didn't matter. If our trip taught me anything, it's that a father doesn't have to be smart or talented or otherwise remarkable to have a huge impact on a kid's life; he just has to stay involved. For boys of a certain age, a bad day with their dad is better than a good day without him.

We started socializing a little once Peter got out of high school, camping now and then or just having dinner. On an expedition to Mount Rainier in 2009, we spent a week together in a little tent, which revived long-suppressed memories of the Stench Bucket. "You're smelly," he'd say each evening in the same sweat-soaked climbing shirt as he hung up the same festering socks a foot above my head. It felt like old times.

My daughter, Hannah, followed Peter's lead in school and treated Bs like other people's boogers. She earned a merit scholarship to Utah State University and graduated in two and a half years, which included a semester in Spain where one professor told her no non-native speaker could possibly pass his course. She aced it along with all the others.

Torie the dog died in May 2013 after a longer life than any deranged animal deserves. Of course, we miss her as we would a limb.

Alison continues to distinguish herself as a friend, wife, and genetic researcher (don't take my word for it; she was Employee of the Year in 2012 at a company with more than three thousand workers). Fortunately for me, she still doesn't understand how lucky I was to meet her.

I stuck it out at the newspaper for three more years until another Mexico trip with my college buddy opened my eyes to how close I was to cracking. With Alison's encouragement, I quit and took a job in sales, and a few months later I started writing for pleasure for the first time in twenty years.

I sold the Dart in 2006, figuring my new clients might not appreciate the torn upholstery and funky smell, but I often find myself reading Internet ads late at night and dreaming of another. I'd drive it from the Bering Sea to Panama, ship it around to Colombia, and head south to the Straits of Magellan. Instead of taking the common Pacific route, I'd go through Venezuela, drop into Brazil, and work my way across the Amazon Basin on the driest dirt roads I could find.

Of course, I can foresee a few hungry days and uncomfortable nights on such a long trip, and I would guess that some of the characters in the rougher backwaters might be on the unsavory side. But all in all, doesn't it sound like a wonderfully mind-expanding educational experience for a young person?

I can hardly wait to have grandkids!

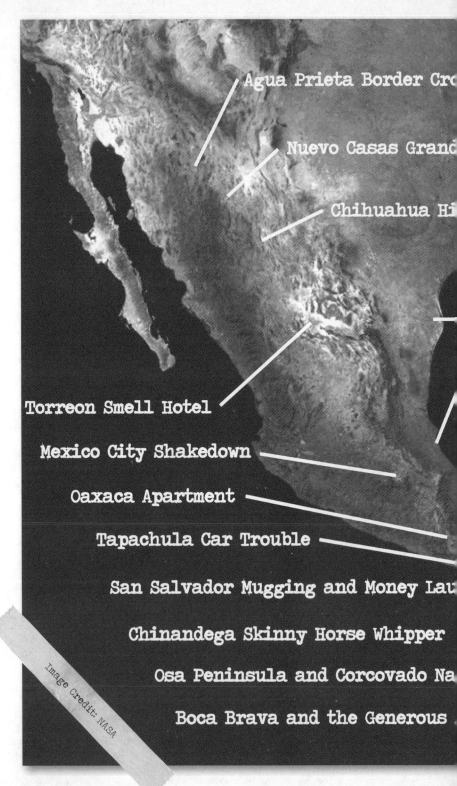

Agua Prieta Border Cro

Nuevo Casas Grand

Chihuahua Hi

Torreon Smell Hotel

Mexico City Shakedown

Oaxaca Apartment

Tapachula Car Trouble

San Salvador Mugging and Money Lau

Chinandega Skinny Horse Whipper

Osa Peninsula and Corcovado Na

Boca Brava and the Generous

Image Credit: NASA

JOURNEY TO THE END OF THE ROAD

...ille Border Crossing

...Hag Magnet Night

...uetzaltenango (Xela) Apartment

Las Lajas Beach Babes

Chitre Camera Thieves

Isla de Taboga Schoolgirl Stalkers

...rk

Yaviza and the End of the Road

9,000 MILES OF CHANGES

When we left in September, Peter
was a slouching little kid.

By December he was a square-shouldered rock star who sparked a girl riot in Oaxaca.

ACKNOWLEDGMENTS

This story would not have become a book without the troopers who read the early drafts. Thank you, Elizabeth Gillenwater, Heather Kenihan, Genevieve Pont, Brian MacIntyre, Cliff Drozda, Millie Drozda, David Millson, Hannah Millson, Doug Nelson, Gil Gillenwater, Ann Poore, Michael Nakoryakov, Pete Lozancich, and Annie Crisp. Without your encouragement, I'd have given up. Without your criticism, I'd have never improved.

Thank you, Michael C. Lewis, author of *To the Brink: Stockton, Malone and the Utah Jazz's Climb to the Edge*, for spotting the clunky phrases the rest of us missed. Thanks also to Troy Gillenwater for two careful reads, and for taking the iconic photo of Peter, me, and the Dart that appears on the cover.

A big thanks to acquisitions editor Haley Miller, who went to bat for a book that didn't exactly fit the publisher's business model, to Angela Baxter for her spectacular cover design, and to the rest of the talented Cedar Fort team who took it from there.

I'm especially grateful to my patient wife, Alison, who has read every word of every draft of everything I've written with contagious enthusiasm. I try never to think of where I'd be without her.

And finally, thank you everyone who has blown a few valuable hours reading this story. I sincerely hope you enjoyed it. If so, you can see more photos at 9000miles.net and find out what's next.

Safe travels.

ABOUT THE AUTHOR

S even moves in seven years as a pre-teen cursed Kirk Millson with a pathologically low tolerance for routine. After terrorizing his wife, Alison, with several near-death wilderness experiences, he toughened up his young children on a steady diet of desert excursions until their luck changed and his career intervened. Currently free of the restrictions of corporate America, Kirk eagerly awaits some grandchildren with whom he can resume his backcountry ramblings. He and Alison live in Salt Lake City.